# YANKEE STOREKEEPER

## By R. E. GOULD

*Illustrated by Stephen J. Voorhies*

Full of Yankee wisdom and wry humor, a foxy old storekeeper sits back and tells of his four decades running a general store up in Somerset County, Maine. It is a tale well stocked with horse sense and chuckles, picturing a grand institution, and a full life that is gradually disappearing from the American scene.

R. E. Gould got his first taste of trading on his father's farm, where his days were spent in trapping, soap-making, a vigorous country boy's life. But when the time came to set up his own store, he soon found that life wasn't all striped candy. One minute he'd be strutting like a turkey gobbler over a good sale and the next he'd be wondering how to pay the next month's bills.

In those days, the country storekeeper had to comb the corners of the earth for his customers and be ready to supply them with everything from pink salmon from Alaska to pink corsets from Paris, from rocking chairs to wrist watches. He clothed the town's children, fed them and their houses when they grew up; he end he buried them, for Gould town's only and therefore its " mortician.

gh the years Gould became a observer of the life around him— human nature and had a hard ith a penny. He even was forced ean and ornery at times to keep rt city drummers and chain stores hooting the corners" off his establ t. In his own words, a country eper "had to have the power of , the patience of Job, and the wis- a jury of Solomons."

tells of the queer characters of every small town has its quota; he Dollar Day Sales and preparing Annual Firemen's Muster; of all ks of the game, when a man's first ad to be right and trading was a dventure.

YANKEE STOREKEEPER will make you long for the days when a country store had big buckets of Mulberry mixture on hand, heavy ripe cheese out of a barrel, a fat tub filled with molasses, Congress boots and calico, when a man could enjoy being his own master — if he had the time.

# Yankee Storekeeper

By R. E. GOULD

Whittlesey House
McGraw-Hill Book Company, Inc.
New York      London

YANKEE STOREKEEPER

*Copyright*, 1946, by CURTIS PUBLISHING CO.
*Copyright*, 1946, by R. E. GOULD

All rights reserved. This book, or parts thereof, may not be reproduced in any form without permission of the publisher.

First Printing

*This book is produced in full compliance with the government's regulations for conserving paper and other essential materials.*

PUBLISHED BY WHITTLESEY HOUSE
A division of the McGraw-Hill Book Company, Inc.

Printed in the United States of America

## CONTENTS

1. A Bargain, B'God — 1
2. My Mean Disposition — 9
3. My First Sale — 22
4. My Apprenticeship — 25
5. I Go on the Road — 36
6. General Trading — 43
7. My Parental Inheritance — 49
8. My First Store — 59
9. Prunes for Sawmills — 65
10. Potatoes — 79
11. Credit, Going and Coming — 83
12. Going After It — 93
13. First and Second Guesses — 96
14. I Pay to Advertise — 101
15. The Board of Education — 114
16. I Catch a Thief — 121
17. Cost Marks and Selling Prices — 127

## CONTENTS

| | | |
|---|---|---|
| 18. | Queer Characters | 134 |
| 19. | God's People | 142 |
| 20. | Grangers | 153 |
| 21. | Undertaking | 160 |
| 22. | Corn Bread, etc. | 169 |
| 23. | Co-ops and Chain Stores | 181 |
| 24. | Two Percent, Ten Days | 188 |
| 25. | The Old Orders Change | 191 |

# Yankee
# Storekeeper

## A BARGAIN, B'GOD

Nostalgic memories of the old days, I'm afraid, haven't bothered me across a broad front. I have my sentimental memories, but somehow I have never repined about leaving the old farm at such an early age. If I have ever amounted to anything as a trader, I suppose I should be sorry I didn't stay home longer, because father was certainly a grand teacher on this subject. No doubt he was much like others in the neighborhood, because trading and swapping was more than a livelihood there. It was an emotional safety valve, perhaps—maybe the Yankee Puritan's substitute for gambling. A trading character, anywhere in Maine, is often a pitiful figure as he tries to keep in hand all the loose ends of his many transactions. Trade today, and someone is trying to get even with you tomorrow. My father was a trading character, and when he crossed the path of another trading character there was plenty for a small boy to learn about dickering.

My father once sold a horse. The horse was absolutely worthless, and he dressed up the window like this: He said,

## A BARGAIN, B'GOD

"Now you see that horse. He looks all right; got a good mouth, legs all right, nice color, clever as a sheep. But he's got faults and I don't like him, and I am selling him on account of them. Now I might have lied to you and told you he was all right and maybe fooled you. But I won't lie. Now this horse has got two faults. I'll tell you one before we trade, and if we trade I'll tell you the other."

The other man asked what the first fault was, and father said, "He's awful hard to catch." If the horse was turned out to pasture, it took all the neighbors to get a hand on him. The answer to this was easy—don't turn him out; and as the price was reasonable the man agreed to trade. After he had paid his money he asked father what the second fault was. Father shoved the bills into his pocket and said, "He ain't good for nothin' when you catch him."

Father's chief opponent was an extremely profane man. Any old resident will remember him—he was called Horace by God. He dealt in anything that had a trading value, and some things that didn't. He bought and sold timber lots and wood lots. He dealt in cattle. He bought wool and hides. He attended auctions and bought wagons which he left in his fields surrounded by horse rakes, sleds, pungs, and anything else that came to hand. "As big as Horace b'God's wagon shed" meant all outdoors. He would sometimes lie and one frequently had to make allowances. Father and Horace by God went through life evening their scores.

Once Horace got father with both barrels at close range. The wheels on father's ox-cart were getting old, and one day one of them gave up the ghost in a ditch under a load. The

## A BARGAIN, B'GOD

approach was open enough. Father said, "What've you got for a set of cart wheels?"

Horace said, "Got just what you want by God. Got them up to Jonathan Jordan's auction by God. The last pair that old man Robinson made by God, and they're worth $25 anyone's money by God. You look 'em over."

One was in good shape, and father asked to see the other. Horace was milking. He said, "Them damned boys run some straw on it when we was thrashin'. Take that fork and dig." Father pitched straw but couldn't find it. Horace said, "You dig in a little, and by God you'll find it."

But father couldn't, and as he only wanted one wheel he finally swapped a breachy heifer for the pair and made Horace promise to bring the other one around when he found it. Horace took a load of straw over to the hotel a few days later, and he brought the wheel around. It wasn't worth a cent. From that time on, father laid traps for Horace, by God.

One afternoon a shower was coming up. We had just got the last load of hay in the barn when Horace came down the road with his old horse on the run and turned into our barn doors just as the heavens opened. "Just made it, by God," said Horace as the thunder rolled and rattled.

"Where you going?" asked father, looking in the back of the wagon at a fair-looking sheep with her legs tied.

"Going down to Frank's with this damned cosset. I got her of Ves Merrill and she gets back through the stump fence to be with the cattle. Damned cosset, by God."

"What'll you take for her?"

"Two dollars, by God."

## A BARGAIN, B'GOD

She looked to be well worth it, but father was a trader. He said, "I'll give you a dollar and a half."

Horace said, "It's a bargain, by God. It's worth a half-dollar to drive down to Frank's."

After the shower I drove out to the pasture with the sheep and turned her loose. I went for the cows after supper and found the sheep in our oats. No wonder she was fat. I tried to drive her to the barn to put a fetter on her, but she evaded me in a twinkling and cleared the fence at a bound. No deer ever jumped better. For two weeks I was busy trying to catch that sheep. We got the neighbors to join the chase, but no luck. I had read how Indians will run down a deer, and I decided to try to run this lady down. A sheep is short-winded, and I got her after an hour of steady running. I tied her and fettered her, and in the fall she graced our table in the form of mutton. Father told someone about her, and learned that a man had given her to Horace to be rid of a nuisance. That called for setting more traps.

Horace sometimes peddled meat, and one day he offered father a choice cut for two dollars. Father bought it for seventy-five cents and Horace left it at the house as he drove by. When we got home, mother was whittling at the piece of meat and raving. She said, "Don't you ever buy any meat from Horace again—this is filthy!"

Father upbraided Horace about this, and Horace came in to make his peace with mother. He swept off his hat and said, "Little hoss dung on that meat, was they, Mis Gould? Wouldn't wonder, wouldn't wonder, by God. Had it wrapped in a hoss blanket."

Laying traps for Horace often consumed some time and

## A BARGAIN, B'GOD

was not necessarily planned over the whole period. I remember once that we got him good. A man tried to sell father an old boar. Such a chattel is of precious little value—no one loves him. The man allowed he was ready to give him away, practically, and he would take ten dollars for him. Father, who knew the boar situation as well as the next man, also knew that the ten dollars was merely conversation. Father seldom paid money for anything. He said, "I'll give you a pig for him."

Pigs were down to $1.50 that fall, and the only prospect he met had offered him six dollars for a litter of ten. The boar vender was indignant and left our dooryard in a fine pique. He came back the next day and accepted the offer. The boar had a bad disposition, and had made a pass at the hired man, cleaving his leg with a tusk. The flesh wound was slight and would heal, but the pants were a total loss and the hired man was mad about it. He said he would kill the boar. A live pig seemed like a lot more than a dead boar, so father and I went down to collect our swap.

Neighbors of ours always wandered what power father had over the hog kind. The hired man climbed up on the great beams of the barn when father knocked down the boar pen. The boar came out, and father drove him home, unleashed, with a small switch. He went along peacefully enough, and walked into our barn as pretty as you please. Father threw down some corn, and while the boar occupied himself with this treat he made a noose with some rope. He slipped the noose around one of the boar's hind legs and attached the rope to a set of pulley blocks. In a minute we opened the scuttle and lowered Mr. Hog down head first. When he was

## A BARGAIN, B'GOD

at the right height father performed a surgical operation that completely changed his character and cut the rope and let him go.

For six months the boar lived under our barn and ate all and sundry that came his way. His appetite was wonderfully prolific and his avoirdupois responded nobly. Along toward the end of the fattening process he would eat a half-bushel of meal one day and three pecks the next. He weighed about five hundred pounds when father got ready to cash in on him.

He sold the lean meat to a German butcher who came up and conducted the funeral. The lean meat on an old stag like this is fairly good, and the money that changed hands was considerable. And we had a barrel of salt pork left. The pork on such a hog is not capable of underestimation. It was about five inches thick, of which three inches was rind. It was probably the most indestructible barrel of pork ever salted. We put it in the cellar, and finally Horace stepped into the trap.

Horace had an old sow that had run in the slaughter house pen and proved to be in an interesting condition. Some one had told Horace a sow that had been eating slaughter-house waste would kill her pigs, and he set about remedying this defect. He began by trying to sell her to father.

Father said, "I'll swap you a barrel of pork for her." Horace examined our barrel of pork in the dim light of our cellar. He asked, "Is it all like this?" and was assured it was. They traded, and father rushed over and brought the sow home. She had seventeen pigs and of course she mothered her little ones lovingly and well. Since nature had not furnished her seventeen places at the table, three of us children had little pigs to bring up on bottles. All seventeen lived long enough

## A BARGAIN, B'GOD

to become assets, and the old sow herself was sold on her past record for $25.

Once father reminded Horace, "You cheated me on a pair of cart wheels."

Horace said, "What did you do to me on that damned pork, by God? Never sold none of it. I wore it all out, by God, hauling it around."

Father said, "You must have given it quite a ride."

So I suppose I come from trading people, and found myself equipped with a natural talent that stood me well in the store. I have often felt sorry for the managers of chain stores, who do business for set prices that are as unalterable as the laws of the Medes and Persians. I have always carried certain articles in stock, specially priced to allow for dickering when someone wants to trade. Sometimes I took a licking, and sometimes I didn't.

## 2

## MY MEAN DISPOSITION

I MUST have been five or six when father took me trading with him, and we visited a store in Lisbon village. Father and the storekeeper talked prices for a time, and then the storekeeper put out a little bait. He went behind the counter, opened a jar, and gave me a penny stick of striped candy. It must have been the first candy I ever tasted. I decided soon after that, maybe at that moment, that I would own a store when I grew up.

I grew up. My first job away from home was in a store. I've owned more than one. And it hasn't all been striped candy. As I look back I see little to attract anyone into the business. The hours are long and the work is confining. A man needs the power of Samson, the resourcefulness of Napoleon, the determination of Grant, the patience of Job, and the wisdom of a jury of Solomons. And then he may fail if he doesn't separate the sheep from the goats and recognize early in life that his customers are divided into two classes. Those who pay cash and don't want to let him make a profit, and those who ask for credit and often do not pay at all. Work-

## MY MEAN DISPOSITION

ing the middle against both ends more often dwindles your funds, but everyone thinks you are growing rich. Customers who haggle you down on prices whittle away at your income, and every drummer who comes in will shoot the corners off by trying to sell you more than you can afford of things you shouldn't buy at all. And still people go into the store business. I guess they must like it. I know I did.

The intelligent country storekeeper is the purchasing agent for his community. Every day he watches the markets to see what he can buy and when he can buy it best—and he makes his decisions in terms of what his community wants. Under his one roof he assembles salmon from Alaska, tea from India, spices from the Orient, sugar and pineapples from wherever he can get them, oranges from California, figs from Smyrna, dates from Arabia, and cheese from Holland. He combs the markets of the world to tempt your appetites and satisfy your tastes. He has radios and hardware, clothing and shoes, crockery and glassware, dresses for old and young—and prices right. And when at last he lays down the reins his heirs or his creditors step in and wind up his affairs and kick because he didn't leave more.

But not always. I have in mind a country store at Farmington Falls, where the name Croswell Brothers has been over the door for nearly two centuries. Always two brothers have succeeded to the business, and always they have been successful. I have long admired that store and have enjoyed stories of how the various brothers have brushed off too persistent salesmen. I know what that means, because when *Grocers' Magazine* asked me to write an article on "What trait is most

## MY MEAN DISPOSITION

needed to succeed in business?" I answered, "A mean disposition."

I know, and the Croswell Brothers know, that the world regards as a mean disposition the simple rebuff of a smart storekeeper who says no and means it. The salesman is hired and trained to oversell the storekeeper, and the storekeeper is cutting his own throat if he's nice to them. Between specialty salesmen and delinquent debtors a storekeeper's choice of words is sometimes sulphured like bleached oats.

Once a storekeeper's disposition is sufficiently mean to handle salesmen, he finds the debtor a bigger problem. Of course, he can do as chain stores do and sell only for cash. The joker in this is that the chain stores actually do a tremendous amount of credit business. If you are a good customer of a chain store, and ask for credit, you will probably get it. To be sure, the manager of the store makes the amount good if you never pay, but the poor devil is driven so hard by the chain to get more business that he takes that chance. A credit customer who pays is ahead of a cash customer. He is yours forever and ever, amen. He never questions prices, and if he pays he is as good as a farrow cow. Of course, if he doesn't pay you have to go after him, and there goes some more sulphured language.

After many years' experience in general stores here and there, I found myself standing in the middle of a new place at Anson, Maine, on the first of June, 1920. I bought the place with an option to take over anytime up to the first of July. As I figured, the former owner started a closing-out sale, and he got rid of a lot of junk I didn't want to buy. When

## MY MEAN DISPOSITION

he began dropping prices on the things I wanted, I jumped in and yelled whoa. The place was mine.

Anson is just across the Kennebec River from the thriving mill town of Madison, and the store used to be the center for a prosperous business with farmers who drove in from miles around. But the man who retired from the business had sold to a storekeeper who had no sign whatever of a mean disposition. This new owner soon found a store full of goods he couldn't sell, a register full of accounts he couldn't collect, a clerk who was strongly suspected of tapping the till, and two expensive delivery routes.

The routes were losing money because the drivers were letting the customers buy what they wanted. Unless the drivers of routes like this really sell goods, the customers will buy advertised items, and advertised items are sold by the chains as loss leaders and don't carry any profit. I thought I had the cure all figured out and could put the store back on its feet. I had bought at a big discount, and although prices were high they were beginning to show signs of crumbling after the war. The store was loaded with old goods bought when prices were low, but where the previous owner couldn't sell them I thought I could, and I planned to use the accumulation to help me down off the top shelf.

I was directing a force of clerks. One man was washing windows. Two were swamping out under the counters. One man was carrying to the dump a wagonload of discarded winter clothing that had been piled on a counter since I don't know when. I was trying to think of ways to get the ball rolling when an automobile drove up out front and seven drummers got out. Some of them I'd seen before—they were

## MY MEAN DISPOSITION

specialty salesmen and they were here to skin me to my last cent. They had heard a new man was going into business, and that was where they got in their best licks. Many a storekeeper has been ruined by unwise buying in the first few weeks, but not me—I already had my mean disposition. I took my entire supply off the shelf and waited for the first drummer, with both barrels loaded to the muzzle.

"I am the Cottolene man," he said. "How is your stock?"
I said, "I've got plenty."
He asked, "How much have you?"
I said, "None."

He began to tell me the great business I was losing by not having it in stock, and I told him I wasn't going to be the goat and hold the bag for a misguided attempt to sell cottonseed oil at a high price by advertising.

"Somebody has been lying to you about me," I told him. "I'm not as foolish as I look."

The next sold tobacco. He wanted me to buy a new kind of cigarette. I said, "I can't sell them." He said he had a nice new tobacco, too. I said, "I don't want it." He said, "If you buy a thousand cigarettes I'll give you two plugs of tobacco."

I said, "Why should I buy cigarettes I can't sell to get tobacco I don't want?" The way I was feeling that day, I could sell anything I wanted to sell, for something, but breaking in a new cigarette is too time consuming. The profit on each sale is small, and all stores use them as leaders.

Some of the drummers just visited, because I knew them before. I showed them around and explained I wasn't buying anything until I got straightened around. The toughest of the bunch were the Salada Tea and the Ivory Soap man. At

## MY MEAN DISPOSITION

that time manufacturers had the idea they could sell anything by advertising it. Then they'd sell the storekeeper a deal so large it tied up too much capital. Not only that: they usually dumped carloads in the chains, and we'd see the chain store windows plastered with prices lower than our cost. Sulphured language again. The Ivory Soap man was rarin' to go. He let me have both barrels, and I couldn't get a word in for some time. Then I said, "I'm not going to handle your soap."

He laughed at me. He said, "Your trade will demand Ivory and P&G soap."

"What good'll that do 'em if I don't have it?"

"They'll go elsewhere, man!"

I had a different idea. I told him I could afford to lose the trade that would leave me on that account, and that I'd do business with the rest on a substitute. "It'll sell just as well, and after I get 'em using it, you'll be the one out of luck." That's just what happened, too.

This condition isn't so bad now. Too many retailers saw the handwriting on the wall and refused to stock advertised goods and the manufacturers had to protect their retailers.

The Cream Corn Starch man came next. I said, "I have enough."

"How much've you got?"

"Fifteen packages; that'll last me fifteen weeks, anyway."

He said, "We have a deal; you buy five cases and we give you one."

I said, "Any man who buys five cases of cornstarch is crazy."

He said, "I've just come out of Aroostook County, and every dealer buys twenty-five cases."

## MY MEAN DISPOSITION

I said, "In Aroostook all the eggs and milk are shipped in, and women have to use cornstarch. This is Somerset County where we raise milk and eggs, the women don't use it, and I won't buy it."

He said, "I only come once a year."

I said, "So do taxes, and I don't care if I never see either of you again."

He tried to make me promise I'd buy his product when my supply ran out. I said, "I won't promise that, but I'll promise never to buy any more when this is gone." And I never have.

Then he paid me a great tribute. He said to one of the other drummers as he went out, "This son-of-a-bitch is tougher than that bastard at Farmington Falls." When I heard of it I felt as if I had been awarded a diploma. I knew that my mean disposition was adequate, and all I had to worry about were bad bills.

Just as my mean disposition was hitting a new high, the Arm and Hammer man spiked me. He smiled pleasantly and said, "I know you're not ready to buy, Mr. Gould, so here's my card, and when you're ready I'll be glad to hear from you." He's heard from me often, and probably smiles when other salesmen relate how tough I am.

I turned again to arranging my stock. The second floor was jammed with goods that probably went back ten years. I had bought ten kinds of soap I never heard of, and there were twenty-five chests of tea that the previous owner had bought at a job lot for eight cents a pound. I nodded my head with pleasure at the things I could do with eight-cent tea, but

## MY MEAN DISPOSITION

when I figured closer I found that my discount on the entire stock gave me that tea a good deal cheaper than that. The varieties were congou, young hyson, and several I'd never met before. All through the place I found items that called for original ideas, and I wandered around rigging up schemes.

I began to help the drivers put up their orders. I found they were selling a P&G soap at three bars for a quarter, when it cost seven and three-quarters cents. I asked what that meant, and the driver said, "The A&P sells it for that." I blew up. "If you think you're working in an A&P, turn in your book and get off that wagon. I'm not paying you $28 a week to meet A&P prices on credit. Let them buy that soap where they please, and you sell them the soap we've got!"

I rushed upstairs and looked over my prize packages. I found a soap that cost me two cents a cake, and put a price on them of eight for twenty-five cents, and we began to do business. We sold four cases the first day, and the boys found they could sell things as well as take orders. This gave me a lift, too, and after a few similar stunts I went to work on my tea.

The store had been selling advertised brands. Tea cost fifty-eight cents a pound and sold for thirty-two cents for a half-pound because the A&P sold it for that. Coffee was costing twenty-nine cents and sold for thirty-three cents for the same reason. I was loaded for fair on tea. I found a chest of Formosa and with that as a base I mixed several different blends that had a fair sampling at my own table. I finally decided on two blends that promised well and I had some bags printed. The bag said,

## MY MEAN DISPOSITION

"One-half pound Rose (or Mayflower) blend tea blended and packed by R. E. Gould, Anson, Maine. If not satisfactory return the empty bag and get your money. That's the way I do business."

The tea cost me so little I wasn't afraid of the refund, and it was only by giving my conscience the cold shoulder that I forced myself to put a price of twenty-five cents a bag on it. We were off again.

A bill came in for a hindquarter of beef at twenty-eight cents a pound. I figured the prices for each cut, the proportion of waste, and told the meat cutter he was losing $5 on every quarter he cut up. He said he knew it. "Well, why don't you get some native beef?" His answer was that we couldn't sell the forequarter stuff. It is perfectly true that God made beef for a variety of tastes, and put it all on one set of feet, but I always figured he gave me a brain to figure out what to do about it. I figured I could sell meat wherever it grew, and we bought native beef.

Village women want something they can fry and save fuel, and we were selling meat to village women. The answer was simple—sell meat to country people, too. Country people have plenty of fuel, and like boiled beef. I loaded a truck with meat, put in a few groceries including my blended tea, and toured the countryside three afternoons a week. I could buy native beef to cost twelve to fifteen cents a pound, and we sold both ends. I also opened up a valuable source of supplies for such items as eggs, butter, berries, vegetables, hogs, et cetera. I made the first few trips to get the thing going right, because I wanted all my drivers to think along the same line

## MY MEAN DISPOSITION

I did. A little old lady bought a bag of tea, and I told her if she didn't like it to bring me the empty bag on Tuesday and get her quarter back.

Tuesday, there she was with her bag. I put on the brakes and pulled out a quarter. "Mr. Gould," she said, "Have you any more of that tea? It's the best I ever tasted, and my daughter wants five packages." From then on I knew my ground on tea, and thought I knew it on all the goods I pushed.

Vanilla fooled me for a few days. In came a shipment of five gross of vanilla extract. I asked what was the idea in tying up money in that quantity of extract. The clerk said, "That won't last two weeks. We sell a lot of it. We get thirty-five cents for it when they cook with it, and forty cents when they drink it. The dealers have all agreed on that price."

I said, "You damned fool, do you want to go and live in the brick house at Skowhegan? If you ever repeated that in the presence of an officer, salt wouldn't save you. Never let me hear that again. Stop all such sales immediately."

Right after that a French-Canadian came in and asked for two dozen bottles of vanilla. The clerk said he couldn't sell it, except for cooking. The customer said, "Das all right, my wife he's gon make a hell of a big Nova Scotia cake, and she want him." It's too bad to hold up a cake like that, but it was held up. Then I got a formula and put up my own vanilla—you could drink a washtub full and never hiccough. It went on sale, and I guarantee it all went for cooking.

I kept on, down one row of shelves and up the other, looking over the stock and thinking of things to do. I found a shelf loaded with cholera cure and louse powders. One of the

## MY MEAN DISPOSITION

first things I found was a pile of hides the previous owner had bought—they smelled as if the funeral should have been held the week before. I found a hundred bags of stock feed. Someone who couldn't say no had bought a carload in twenty-five-pound bags. This had cost a lot, but when the man waked up to his situation he jobbed out a lot of it for anything he could get; but Mr. Willis found it just as hard to sell as before. It cost me with discount off about two cents a pound. I knew the formula for stock feeds in general and probably this one. The formula was,

|  |  |
|---|---|
| 1200 lbs. | Linseed Meal |
| 400 lbs. | Epsom Salts |
| 100 lbs. | Ginger |
| 100 lbs. | Salt |
| 100 lbs. | Fenugreek |
| 100 lbs. | Charcoal |
| 2000 lbs. | |

I made up a dairy ration out of ground oats, corn meal, linseed meal, cotton seed, gluten, and so on, and to every ton I added a generous supply of stock feed. I could get $80 a ton for my cow feed, so my stock feed turned at a profit. To my surprise cows fed on my dairy ration topped the creamery in yield per cow for several months.

One of the front counters held a display of jewelry. The former owner kept it padlocked, and he took the key out and showed me how it worked. He locked and unlocked the padlock, then made me work it. When he had finished, I unlocked the padlock and put it in my pocket, leaving the jewelry case open.

## MY MEAN DISPOSITION

"You mustn't do that," he gasped.

I asked why not, and he said, "They'll steal it."

I said, "I hope they do, that's the best way I know of to get rid of it."

A man came in a short time afterward and asked my price on a watch chain. I said, "What'll you give?" He said he had offered $4 for it, "but A. B. said he couldn't put it back for that."

I said, "I'm not going to put it back, give me the money."

After I had done everything I could think of to get the stock in shape, the good Lord took a hand. I was out in the country with the meat truck, and a bolt of lightning visited me while I was away. The small blaze in the basement gave the firemen a good workout, and they squirted extinguishers all over my canned goods. The insurance covered any possible loss I might have sustained by falling prices. I figured I then had everything under control, and it was time to run my first sale.

## 3

## MY FIRST SALE

Dollar day sales are common in all communities, but I know I put on the craziest one ever devised. I had so much unsalable junk that I announced a huge dollar day sale—a dollar day that was to be all my own without any other merchants joining in. I began by getting down my square packages of poultry louse powder, which actually did sell for a dollar when people bought it. I found some cotton sweaters that also sold for a dollar, but no man in town was old enough to remember when. I had old-style women's shoes, corsets of a fetching salmon pink, and odds and ends that had accumulated through years of careless buying and through failure to have periodic sales.

I really ran a sort of grab-basket sale. Everything was wrapped up, and the terms of the sale stipulated no refunds or exchanges. I also said no package would be of a retail value under one dollar, and could have proved it. We wrapped the bundles so they were properly disguised, and each was marked one dollar. One sweater would be wrapped in a compact

## MY FIRST SALE

bundle. The next would be rolled around a stick. A third would be put in a big box. And so on through the whole sale stock. I stipulated some of the items—100 pounds of sugar, 98 pounds of flour, suit of clothes, boys' suits, ladies' shoes, and a grand prize of a 9 x 12 art square that had sold for $28. The bigger items were indicated by tickets wrapped to look like louse powder, pink corsets, et cetera. Three coffee percolators that had been selling for $2.50 were put on top of the pile of louse powder, and the first three customers were so pleased that we got rid of a lot of louse powder quickly.

The sale had enough of the unusual about it to bring about everyone into the store at some time during the day. The 9 x 12 art square was still unsold, and the interest kept high. A little Slavic girl, Mary something or other, had been doing a lot of buying, and she finally got the art square. I saw her talking with her mother, and she took my fancy because she was so clever about figuring out my disguises. She had already outfitted a number of her brothers and sisters by cannily picking the right package. She now wanted another dollar for one last buy.

The mother couldn't speak English, and Mary was enough of a Yankee now to make up for it. The mother clung to the dollar, but Mary was persistent. Quite a dispute followed, and Mary at last got the dollar. She handed it to me and pointed at a package of louse powder—at least as far as anyone in town knew, save myself, it was louse powder. It was actually a louse powder box, with the contents dumped out and the ticket for the art square in it with some corn meal to make it weigh. Mary insisted on one special package. I handed

## MY FIRST SALE

it to her. The youngster was cute, bright-eyed, sweet and lovely, and I said, "That's the art square."

Mary said, "I thought it was, it would be the last package anyone would take."

I said, "I'll have the art square delivered first thing in the morning."

Sweet little Mary said, "Not by a goddam sight, we'll take it home now." And Mary and her mother shouldered the rug on a long pole, and trudged down the street in the gathering gloom. My first sale was over, and I locked the store door with nearly all my junk disposed of.

## 4

## MY APPRENTICESHIP

In my various storekeeping experiences, I have always been different from the usual run of merchant. One customer once told me, "You're so contrary that if you fell in the river, I'd look for you upstream." Now that I'm old and can view life with a perspective, I can see that I have been different, and I can see why. First was my upbringing up on a rocky hill farm by thrifty and canny parents, and secondly was the accident of my first job.

When I was sixteen my father and I frequently disagreed as to who was the boss, and I left home. It was an easy thing to find work on a farm, and I had several choring jobs before I landed in a store at Lowell, Massachusetts. That wasn't my idea of a good place, so I watched the ads in the Boston Sunday papers, and answered one that was looking for a store clerk. I said I had worked in a store some and had liked it, and that I was a good worker. If I were applying for a job today, I'd say about the same thing.

I got a telegram a day or so later, asking me to go to Portsmouth, New Hampshire, for an interview—expenses paid. I

## MY APPRENTICESHIP

went down and found the old Globe Grocery Store full of strange goods and a lot of smart-looking clerks waiting on a throng of customers. The proprietor was out, and I passed the time inspecting the place. He soon came in bearing about a wheelbarrow load of letters in his arms, and he came directly to me, calling me by name, and asking me to come into his office. I suppose, now, that he was one of the shrewdest merchants that ever lived, and both consciously and unconsciously he taught me everything one man can teach another about storekeeping.

He asked me about myself and family, and soon he had turned me inside out. I told him, I remember, that I knew very little about the grocery business. All this time he was opening letters, glancing at them, and tossing them into a big wastebasket. If it looked silly to me then, it was clear within a year, because I was doing exactly the same thing. Eleven months later I was hiring clerks and throwing out the worthless mail.

He said, "Five hundred people answered that ad. Most of them said they knew all about the grocery business. I've worked at it 60 years and know very little about it. When someone works at it six months and knows it all I feel he's too smart to work for me. But you said you didn't know much about it, and I felt I could teach you."

From that time on I have distrusted the man who learns everything in six months, and the boy of twenty who is so good he has a dozen employers for references. If he were that good someone would have kept him. Later I added the man of forty-five who had a good business but gave it up. There must have been a hole somewhere.

## MY APPRENTICESHIP

It was Friday, and I said I was all ready to go to work. The boss said no, Friday was a bad day to begin anything, to wait until morning. So I spent the afternoon watching the clerks and looking the goods over. My eyes stuck out when I heard the head clerk go to the telephone and order a hogshead of molasses from Portland, just like that.

The head clerk broke me in, because the boss left town for a few days' vacation. He called me down for errors and made me feel pretty inferior, after which I took to portering and tried to keep stock on the shelves. I undertook to get the daily shipment of freight, which was huge, stacked in the basement in the proper places. Flour came in barrels, and a barrel of each kind was kept open at the back of the store. If a customer wanted fifty cents' worth, she had to wait while it was put up, so I began bagging small quantities and marking them. These bags were stacked close at hand, and the customer hardly said "Fifty-cents' worth of Ceresota," when there it was before her. In fact, I kept myself so busy that on the fourth day when the boss blew in unexpectedly, I was the only one at work.

Two of the clerks were out on the sidewalk making dates with two of Portsmouth's fairest flowers. The head clerk had taken the day off to go up in the belfry of the North Church to show his girl how his new camera worked. Two were shaking dice down cellar, and another was reading the Portsmouth *Herald*, and customers waiting.

The rattling of the dry bones was something to hear.

Up until then I had seen only the good-natured side of the boss, but here was something else. I thought sure I'd be fired as soon as the boss heard of all the mistakes I'd made. But when he made his regular Saturday night visit to the cash drawer to pay off the help, he gave me half a dollar too much. I discreetly waited until I could speak to him privately, and told him he had overpaid me. He said, "No, you're worth it."

I don't remember stepping on the sidewalk at all going home, and my intense liking for this old man has been something of a guiding star to me ever since. He knew the grocery and retail business from the ground up, and knew all the little side-shows that keep the interest going. I've done many merchandising stunts that he never thought of, but he taught me the rudiments and many of the flourishes.

One day a customer came in and protested that I hadn't put up fifty cents' worth of sugar she had ordered. I distinctly remembered putting it up and was giving her an argument when the boss pushed me aside and said, "We will send up fifty cents' worth of sugar at once. We don't know how it was lost, but we know it wasn't your fault."

After she left, pleased, he turned to me and said, "Never have a row about fifty cents; it isn't worth it." I saw the point, but I still remembered putting up the sugar, so I watched the baskets we put up for the delivery boys, and one day I caught a boy sneaking out with a fifty-cent bag of sugar. His mother would give him a half-dollar for sugar, and he'd save it for another purpose by stealing the sugar from a basket already put up.

Portsmouth was a patent medicine town, and we had at least a thousand items that we sold at a cut price. They were arranged on shelves without any attempt at classification. The prices were in an indexed book, but there was a hunt every time anyone wanted Davis' Sarsaparilla, Haarlem Oil, or Kennedy's Medical Dissolvent. It struck me that I could distinguish myself by learning the location of each and every patent medicine. My dinner hour was from 1:00 to 2:00, and from noon until 1:00 was very quiet. I spent that hour each day for three weeks studying the patent medicines. I learned their locations by name, by the diseases they cured, by the color of the labels, by the sizes of the bottles, and many of them by the bearded physician pictured on the box. I had many opportunities to shine because of this, and no doubt enhanced my future.

Every day the name of the leading clerk was posted, an honor based on the total of the sales he had made yesterday. Mine wasn't there very often, because the older clerks knew the good customers and left me the small buyers. One noon I was there with one other clerk who was reading the paper and a drunken longshoreman came in. He reeled up to the counter, fixed me with his eyes and an effort, and said:

"Take my order. I want a hundred pounds of sugar, two barrels of flour, a tub of lard, ten pounds of salt-fish, five pounds of coffee, a pound of tea, five pounds of pilot bread, et cetera. . . ." It added up to a staggering sum. I had never made such a sale. I could see my name up on the bulletin board tomorrow. I asked, "Where shall I send this?"

He roared, "None of your damned business!" and staggered out of the store. I could have shot him with extreme pleasure. I told one of the drivers about it, and he laughed. "Put the order up," he said, "I know where it goes." The old drunk lived on the waterfront, and was well known for his regular monthly orders. When he got paid off, he'd buy his month's supply of staple groceries before he got too drunk. My name went up the next morning and I strutted like a turkey gobbler.

Speaking of turkeys, I bought a turkey one Saturday night when a number were left over. My wife, who was just beginning to housekeep and was frantically trying to be a good cook for three boarders, was afraid she couldn't roast him right. She tried an oyster dressing, and the bird was delicious. It turned out so well that I would buy one every Saturday night. The turkeys came packed in a barrel, with an old gobbler in the center. He would go hard. Along about ten o'clock Saturday night, if he still remained, the price would go down and I'd buy him for eight cents a pound. We'd eat turkey for days, and the boss would occasionally drop a remark that hinted he knew about it and secretly admired my frugality. The patience of my wife and boarders was certainly more remarkable than the price I paid for meat.

I remember some of the prices—they seem fantastic now. Flour was $2.85 a barrel. We sold pea beans at four quarts for ten cents. All one fall and winter we could buy a box of lambs at four cents a pound. We sold forequarters for five cents and hinds for seven cents; nothing less than a quarter sold. It was a good time for a grocery clerk to set up housekeeping.

My old boss frequently philosophized as he taught me the business. He would say, "When you are weighing out a bag of sugar, or anything else, always have less than the right amount in the bag when you set it on the scales. Then put in a little more to make it weigh right. That always pleases the customer, but if he sees you take out some, it makes him mad."

Davis
SARSPARILLA
Annual
Fair
North
Church
STEPHEN J.
VOORHIES

## MY APPRENTICESHIP

He would say, "I want exact weight. Nothing makes a customer so mad as short weight. But if you give him too much, he thinks you're a fool. He never gives you credit for being generous." I have repeated that to scores of my own clerks in the years since, and it's true, every word of it.

I've always been thankful for what my old boss taught me about tea. We specialized on a pound of tea and a present for fifty cents—the sort of thing that led to the old song about giving away a baby with a pound of tea. The tea was a good grade costing about twenty-three cents, and the presents ranged in price from ten to thirty-three cents. The boss always got full value out of advertising, and his agile mind knew all the ways to advertise. The presents were arranged in piles, and when a customer bought tea we'd pass him a basket of little envelopes. He would draw one. In each envelope was a slip bearing a number. He would look at the slip and say, "Number 41, a kettle." Or a salad bowl, or whatever we had the most of.

One day in the winter a man came in with a rocking chair. It was not too expensively made, and was to retail for about ninety-eight cents. The old man dickered and finally ordered a carload of them to be delivered in August. I thought the old man was off his base, as we said then, but they came, and the final cost was down to thirty-three cents. The old man, in the middle of the winter, had seen far enough ahead to be prepared for the annual Firemen's Muster. In late August this event came around, and it drew at least 10,000 people from out of town. Fire companies from Massachusetts and New Hampshire, and from all of western Maine brought their hand tubs, held a big parade, and competed for big prizes.

## MY APPRENTICESHIP

On this day we gave away a rocking chair with a pound of tea.

If you can picture a carload of rocking chairs loose in that crowd, you can visualize the advertising that store got. I remember looking up the street and seeing a line of fat old women sitting on the sidewalk, comfortably rocking back and forth, and watching the parade—the bag of tea reposing in each lap. I've always wondered how many eyes nearly or actually got punched out as the rockers were taken home on excursion trains.

Another stunt made me gasp for breath, because I didn't believe the public was so gullible. One July the steamer *Venetian* was wrecked going out of Boston harbor. The Boston Sunday papers told the story, and had pictures of men carrying quarters of beef damaged by sea water—and there were advertisements offering this beef at a cut price.

The next morning the old man was missing. He was on a bargain hunt in Boston. He found a dry goods house and bought out a summer dress material, very pretty, originally priced to sell at about twenty cents a yard. They had three cases and he finally got it for eight cents. He had it cut into ten-yard lengths, wrapped in newspapers, and scrambled together as if by incompetent help. He hurried back to Portsmouth and bought a page in the paper, advertising a sale "From the Wreck of the *Venetian*." At 1:00 P.M. the sale opened. At 1:30 the *Chronicle* man made a picture of 2,000 women fighting to get ten yards of this stuff at $1.19 a bundle. Not one woman commented that the *Venetian* had carried only dressed beef.

Behind his back we called the boss Uncle John, but he was

## MY APPRENTICESHIP

no one to take liberties with. He had written rules for nearly every act in the store. The rules demanded our morning presence at 6:30 A.M., and we were through at 9:00 P.M. Saturday the rules kept us there until eleven, and we had one night a week off. One rule was that clerks could buy any item in the store, at cost, but it must be charged and taken from their wages on Saturday night. This seemed a trifling rule, but it was mighty important. Each clerk had a ledger account, and each item was entered. One day Uncle John said to me, "Did the new boys get rooms at the place I sent them?" I said they did.

He said, "Then go over to their rooms, tell the landlady I sent you, and see if they have any Cashmere Bouquet, Cuticura Soap, or Blackstone Cigars."

I found all three items, plus some Uncle John hadn't missed yet, and Saturday night the three boys were paid off, period. The old man always detected the crooks in his employ before they got enough to hurt. Our labor turnover was heavy, and we had a reputation of being a hard store to stay in—but that Saturday night settling of accounts was one of the reasons and the clerks who got caught by it had only themselves to blame. I have used the same scheme all my life in my own stores.

There was fun in the old store, though. The old man never remonstrated so long as customers were not inconvenienced. One gag was to give a new clerk a hammer and nail, and point out a post where he was to drive the nail to hang his coat on. One swat with the hammer revealed that the post was iron, and it would ring about fifteen minutes. I'd been there about four days when I came back and found my frock

## MY APPRENTICESHIP

pockets full of lard, a discovery that amused the older clerks more than it did me. I improved on the trick, and got revenge, by varying with some molasses.

A favorite trick was to let a new clerk take an order from a good-looking girl customer. He would be writing down the order, putting his best foot forward after the manner of his kind, and she would often be coyly assisting his maneuvers. It would look like a romance for sure, when one of the older clerks would walk by and say, in passing, "Your wife wants you to bring home a pound of butter when you come to supper." I was never called upon to rearrange the fabric of such a romance, myself—but I remember how like a devil I felt when I had an opportunity to make the remark.

The time wore on, and I really liked the work. I was too new to storekeeping to see how things were trending, but other eyes than mine must have been open. The head clerk was let go one day for reasons that Uncle John felt were sound. Similar reasons deposed the other clerks who tried to take his place. I still thought myself the little boy of the outfit, and was wholly unready to read the notice that went up one morning:

> In my absence Ralph Gould will be in charge, and is to be obeyed accordingly.
>
> —J. E. R.

## 5

## I GO ON THE ROAD

---

IF I got the groundwork for storekeeping at Portsmouth, I got the training for trading immediately afterward. I took sick after several years, and the doctor gave me my choice: "Get outdoors and get well, or stay in the store and die."

I shook hands with Uncle John and never saw him again. I carried away with me a ring of keys to the old store, duplicates of keys he had. Today, if you visit me, you will hear me jingling them in my pocket. I can tell you what doors they fit, too. Most people have always thought they were coins. Maybe drummers have thought my jingling was a nervous habit, many people have.

I went back to my native Lisbon Falls, Maine, and bought a farm near my father's. I couldn't begin to do the work the farm called for, and I took on a line of farming machinery and bought and shipped hemlock bark. I found that my living was even better than it had been in the store—I made less money, but it cost less to live. And when I was cited the

## I GO ON THE ROAD

second year as high salesman in the state for my farm machinery, it gave me another idea.

Selling farm machinery is a matter of trading. Every farmer needs more, or new, machinery constantly. But he can be sold only what he can pay for. Farm products represent money, but are not always worth money. If I sold a mowing machine and took two heifers in trade, it was my project to get the value of the heifers before I could square my account with the company. What I had learned in the store didn't help me much in a situation like that, but what I had learned as a boy from watching father trade came back to mind. That year, when it came time to settle for my machinery, I found myself with six head of cattle, all heifers, and that much money too little. The agent of the company came and found my machinery gone. I laid my cards on the table. "If you make me pay now, I've got to sell all six heifers. If you let me keep them until April, I can sell three and pay for six. Can't you help me somehow?"

He pointed out that unsold machinery could be carried over until the next season on an interest-free note, and said, "I'm going to carry you over as on hand six harrows." I sold two heifers in June and squared up. This method of calling the kettle black intrigued me, and I thought that maybe that sort of thing could be stretched to my advantage.

I was selling a lot of machinery to farmers, and taking 60- or 90-day notes. The company offered a five percent discount if the machinery were bought for cash. I took a note to the bank and asked if they would discount it, scarcely believing that sort of thing could be done. Of course, the banker said he certainly would. After a few similar discounts

## I GO ON THE ROAD

had been taken, I asked the banker just how far he would go. "What kind of paper will you take?"

He said, "Anything you'll put your name on." I was off, and wished I'd been smart enough to ask before. Today, I know, both banks and business houses are more strict with their terms and time. But after this war I would expect them to loosen up and be more like old times. It takes young men to sell goods, and usually they need credit. In my time an idea, promising actions, and a likely appearance were credit items. Times have changed, but the good times will come again.

One day a competing farm manufacturer offered me the job of assistant sales manager. A better name is Skunk Skinner—derived from the old Yankee admonition to a growing boy, "Skin your own skunks." I didn't know it, but I was hired for several reasons: I was wanted because I was too valuable to their competitor, and I seemed like a good prospect for skinning the skunks caught by other salesmen. All the hard collection, all the difficult jobs, all the heart-breaking details, fell to me. As an implement salesman I found the job was not to my liking, but I did well at it, and am glad it came my way because it taught me a lot about collection, trading, and meeting people.

Typical of my work was a trip to Mooers Forks above Plattsburg, New York, to collect $150. I found the agent who owed this, and he was most cordial. "Why can't you pay?" I asked him, and he gave me a tale of woe about the failure of his customers to pay him. It looked like a dead-end, but I asked, "Don't you hold some unpaid notes?" He said he did, and he pulled about a bushel of them from under the bed. I picked out two that came to $200 and asked if he

## I GO ON THE ROAD

would give me those for a receipt in full. He said sure, and I gave him the receipt and he signed over the notes.

One was a note on a horse that had died. The other was on a sleigh, a robe, and a harness, given by a woman who lived at the end of a road chuck up against the Canadian line, and she owned in both countries. Creditors who sought to attach her stock in one country would arrive just in time to find she had driven the stock across the line. A collector who had dunned her about a bill for a cookstove, just before me, found her rather forthright. She had him arrested for attempted rape, and scared him so he gave her the stove. There was nothing brilliant about my method of getting the notes paid, however. I took them to a lawyer and asked him if he could collect them. He said he could, and he did. The whole thing taught me never to let go too soon.

The real test of my ingenuity came in respect to repairing machinery. I had such good luck smoothing out a man who was mad because his mower wouldn't mow, that I was put to doctoring machines. I not only had to calm down the victim, but leave him contented with our products, and also fix his machine.

One year we had a disease of mower trouble in Maine, and they moved me over from northern Vermont. That was all right with me, because if there's anything to make a Maine man's appetite go bad, it's northern Vermont. I fixed one machine after another and finally landed in the town of Vienna. In Maine, Vienna is pronounced Vy-yenny, but the people I went to see couldn't pronounce it at all. I found a whole family of deaf-mutes, with only one of their number articulate. They owned farms all up and down the road, and

## I GO ON THE ROAD

had bought a mower among them. I found them lined up across a meadow mowing by hand and very mad because the machine had played out.

I made myself known to the one who talked, and then there was a grand waving of arms and fingers. He turned back to me and said, "It's no use, you'll have to take it back." I asked what ailed the mower and learned it wouldn't cut and also made so much noise a neighbor heard it two miles away.

That's all I needed—the old Buckeye Mower had a big bell-shaped gear on the main axle. It fitted into a pinion, then a speed-gear, and in turn drove the crankshaft. This big bell-gear was apt to warp, and the manufacturer actually allowed for this warping by making extra deep teeth on the gear and pinion. But once in a while it would warp too much, and the thing would howl like a lost soul with its tail jammed in the door. The remedy was simply to put on a handful of spacing washers.

I asked to see the machine, and got it jacked up and apart. Then I thought up pretexts to get the deaf-mutes out of range, and when nobody could see I washered the thing up enough to choke the howl. When they came back I was putting it together. I made them try it, and it mowed perfectly, as well as quietly. The father of this silent horde was completely baffled. He followed the machine around the field, pawed at the grass, and when he came back to me he talked with his fingers enough for a sermon. The talking boy turned to me and said, "Father says you can't fool him—you done something when he wasn't looking." Keen as he was, the old man forgot to ask me what it was I did, and what really ailed

## I GO ON THE ROAD

the machine. Even in those days I made it a practice never to volunteer any information.

But whatever I was learning, I was still the goat for a company that hired me chiefly to put me out of business. They sent me into Aroostook County, Maine, a place that they had never been able to crack. Freight rates were so high nothing but carload lots would pay, and nobody could sell a carload of anything. I was supposed to go up there and introduce a new line of manure spreaders. Well, Aroostook has always been a fertilizer section, and most of the farmers could handle all the manure with a wheelbarrow. It just wasn't cow-manure country. I knew some sort of a potato-growing machine was needed, and I drew out a picture of a two-roe horsehoe, a contrivance that would hill up two rows of potatoes at a crack. Our experimental man had one made, and I demonstrated it at Presque Isle before a big crowd. It cost $28 express just to get it there, and I hated to sell it. I thought we had so much tied up in it, it should be kept as a souvenir. But I sold it to a man on a six-months' note. I knew if he paid the idea was good. Six months later he paid and told me the names of six neighbors who wanted them. We began selling them in big lots, and every time we put fifteen or twenty in a car, we'd fill the car up with other implements. Before long we had Aroostock County buying at a great rate.

That was when they shifted me to Washington County. Washington County is all blueberry barrens and sardine factories, and I was good and tired of my work on the road. I blew into Machias of a Saturday night, wondering how anyone could sell farm tools in a county that did no farming, and

## I GO ON THE ROAD

began to talk with a drummer who sat at my table. He asked me why I didn't buy a store, now that I was healthy again.

"There's a place up at Harmony," he said. "An old gent with one arm and an ingrowing disposition is doing a hell of a business, and he wants to sell. They've just built a railroad up to Harmony from Pittsfield, and it looks like a boom for the town. I'll bet you'd fall in love with the place."

I did. I went up Monday with my mind made up. Harmony had a future—at least compared with its past. The store looked like a sure thing. The old man really wanted to sell, and I found that I really wanted to buy. I jingled Uncle John's keys in my pocket, and wrote out a check for $500— a down payment carrying an option to take over any time before June 1. The property thus bargained for included the store, a grist mill, house, and the right to do business on any and all subjects in an area I thought sufficiently large to suit my talents. On the way back to Machias I composed my letter of resignation as Skunk Skinner.

"From now out, I skin my own," I mused.

## 6

## GENERAL TRADING

THE country storekeeper, if he is to be a successful merchant, must be able to deal with any and all, must buy a great many things—must know what to say and must sift a small amount of truth out of a vast pile of lies and must know values of nearly everything. One morning in early summer when business wasn't very rushing, I was hoeing in my garden and thinking how nicely things were growing and what a beautiful world we lived in and was wishing I could do someone a kindness, when a man drove up with a chestnut mare with a new harness on, in a new top buggy, all looking like something out of a Sears & Roebuck catalog. He said, "Gould, I want to sell you this horse. My wife is in the hospital and I have got to have some money. She is a nice young horse just seven years old. I know because I raised her myself. She is all sound and kind and right in every way and I will take $75 for her and she is worth $150 of any man's money."

Now I found out later that the only true thing about this whole statement was that he wanted to sell me that horse.

## GENERAL TRADING

I took a look at the lady and kept on hoeing. I noted that her ears were laid back at a peculiar slant and that she had eyes like a stinking fish, nearly all white, and that scattered over her hide were numerous stripes of white hair that looked to me as if someone had remonstrated with her with a club. I said, "She looks a lot more like $5 than $75," and he hit her a crack with the whip and vanished in a cloud of dust.

I thought I had looked my last upon the chestnut mare, but it was not to be. About a month later the telephone rang and I answered and a voice asked, "Did you tell Harrold that you would give $5 for his chestnut mare?" I said, "No, but I guess I would." He said, "I'll bring her over," and I had a horse. The owner had put her out to pasture and she proved to be breachy. The pasturer demanded that she be removed and because he couldn't do any better, I got her. I couldn't imagine a sound horse that wasn't worth $5, but she was it. Of all the detestable beasts I ever owned she was the undoubted queen. She refused to work single or double. I could drive her at a very slow pace if I didn't feed her any grain, but if she was fed four quarts of oats for a week, no one could drive her. I had had balky horses before and had always found ways to make them useful, but not this lady.

One balky horse that I had owned was cured as far as I was concerned, but he could not be trusted with hired men. I had a neighbor who was disliked by everyone, named S. K. Neversole. One of my hired men went up to a neighbor's one evening and said, "I believe Gould is crazy. He talks to his horses just as if they were men. That horse he calls Josh balked up with me today; he wouldn't work nor let the other one work. I went down and told Gould and he said, 'That

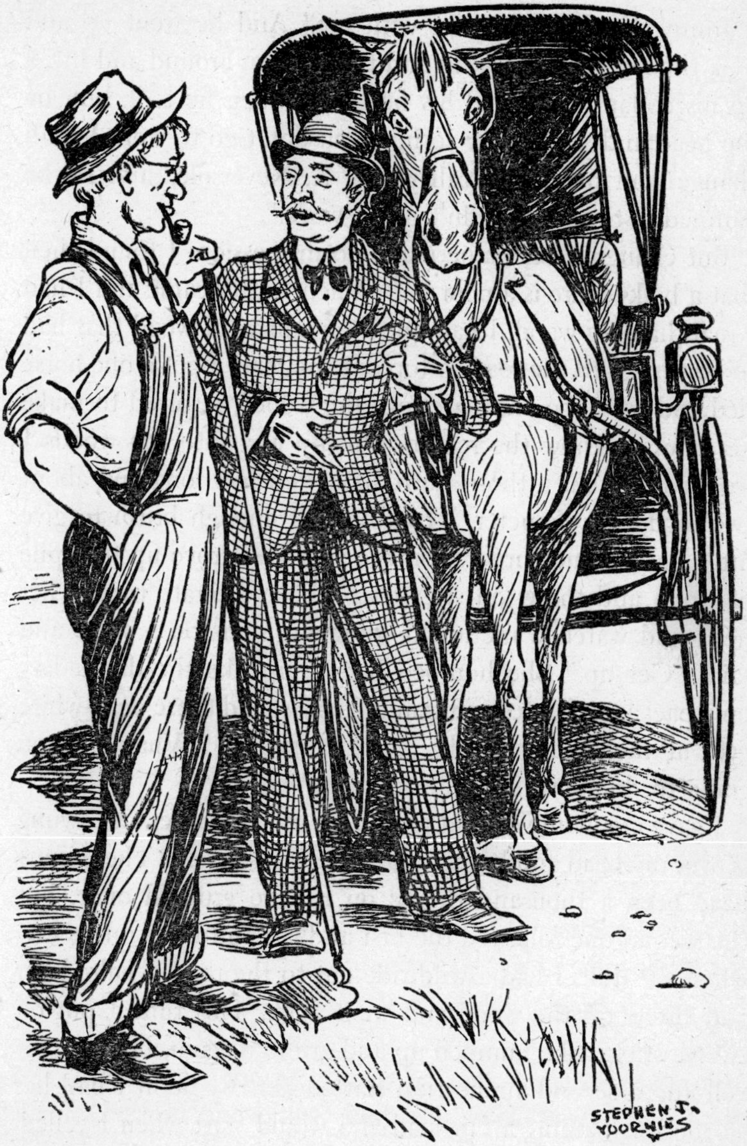
STEPHEN J.
VOORHIES

## GENERAL TRADING

is funny, he don't do that with me.' And he went up and took the horse by the head and turned him around and lifted up his collar and patted his neck, and then he took him by the head and said, 'Now Josh, if you don't go to work I shall change your name and call you S. K. Neversole,' and I'll be damned if the horse didn't go to work."

But changing her name made no impression. I found then that a balky mare is a poor bet. When winter came and I had a man hauling wood, I had quite a quantity of wood that had to be yarded to the road to top out the load. I got a one-horse sled and took the old mare into the woods, resolved to make her haul or know the reason. On my way into the woods I stopped and cut a thorn bush about ten feet long and about two inches in diameter. I trimmed off enough brush to give me a handle and threw it on the sled and drove up to a pile of wood and threw on six sticks. The old pirate turned her head and watched me and I hung the reins on a stake and said, "Get up." She humped herself up like the dromedary on a package of dates and grunted and rolled those dead-white eyes at me, saying in the horse language, "What are you going to do about it?" She soon learned.

I gave an awful yell and picked up my persuader and swung it over my head and brought it down with a crash. There must have been a thousand thorns on it. She grunted once, but the second one followed the first and the third was on its way when she quit. I had a wild ride out to the road. I halted her and threw off the wood and went back. This time I put on twelve sticks. She humped up and grunted again, but another yell and a second application started her. By noon I had her so she was hauling a fair load and would start when I yelled.

## GENERAL TRADING

After dinner I had to use the bush once more, but soon she was working like anyone's horse.

Near my woodpile lived a man with nothing to do except worry about other people's business. He used to come out and talk to me while I was unloading, and he often spoke of what a fine work horse she was. I didn't like to dispute him, but one day I came home and found a horse dealer who told me he wanted a young cheap horse. I told him I had one and led her out. He asked, "What is the story?" and I said, "The man I bought her of said she was seven years old and smooth and sound and a good driver and kind so women could handle her and my wife drives." He asked, "What kind of a worker is she?" and I said, "I wouldn't recommend her as a worker. She isn't built for it. She is a better driver than a worker, still I yarded out that pile of wood with her." He asked the price and I told him $50. He went up and asked my neighbor and got a red-hot recommendation for a work horse. He came back and said, "You have got to shave that price—I am a dealer and I have got to make something." I finally took off ten percent and we traded.

When he drove off with the old mare leading behind he said, "I'll have her looking different in three weeks." The next time I saw him he said, "Gould, you lied to me about that mare." I said, "If I have lied to you in the least degree, I will refund your money and take her back. Now what did I say that wasn't the truth?" He said, "You said she was a good worker." I said, "No, I said I wouldn't recommend her as a worker as she was a much better driver than a worker." He said, "She is no driver at all." I ended, "Have you tried to work her?" He said, "No." I said, "You try that and you will find that I was right." He said, "She balks in a buggy in the stable floor." I said, "You mustn't feed her grain as she can't bear prosperity." Finally he said, "Your neighbor said she was a fine worker." I said, "If I was in your place I would sue him for damages as she never was and I don't think ever will be, but to show that my heart is right, I will give you the thorn bush that I used to stimulate her with before she came out of the woods."

He invited me to go to hell but I was always glad that I told him the truth and if you are going to deal with hardheaded, hard-hearted Yankees, I advise you to go no farther.

# 7

## MY PARENTAL INHERITANCE

I KNOW what it is to skin skunks actually. When I was a boy on the farm Aunt Eunice would occasionally step to the door and sniff. She'd come in and say, "Lizzie, there's an essence peddler around tonight."

She didn't refer to the traveling man who sold extracts, essences, and hair oil by the ten cents' worth, but to a bright-eyed, black-and-white animal the Indians named skunk and meant it. In those days skunk skins were worth from ten to fifty cents, depending on the amount of white on them—the more white the less worth. The ten-cent one predominated, but their power of offensive action was a constant power.

A farm boy could often earn a neat amount of pin money with a string of traps. They were easy to catch. I've heard it said that if anyone sets a trap in the middle of a twenty-acre field, a skunk would find some way to get in it. It was always easy in school to tell which boys tended their traps before classes. A teacher in the Ridge school, in those days, was a martyr to her sense of smell. I always smelled nice, compara-

## MY PARENTAL INHERITANCE

tively speaking, because I never had money enough to buy a few traps to get started.

Then the beneficent Providence that watches over us and grants our reasonable desires noted my plight. The Lisbon Fox Club, composed of the mill agent, a hotel man, the jeweler, the boss of the corn shop, the meat man, and a few others, used to go out in the woods on fall days and hunt foxes in front of a hound, Rover. Rover was a plodding old dog, just about the right speed for these sports. Ladies of the community made slighting remarks about the Fox Club, commenting on the quantity of beverages the members were supposed to consume, but as far as I know none of them died an inebriate's death but prospered and were happy. Happy, that is, until one day Rover died.

One of the members shortly thereafter saw a hound dog advertised in a sporting magazine, and he wrote and inquired the price. The price of $75 struck them as somewhat high, but they were resourceful. They enlarged the club and took in everyone who had a dollar, and when they had 75 new members they wrote and bought Saul's Upland Champion. The new dog arrived and was a beauty. A hunt was organized for the next Saturday.

Old Rover used to move about two miles an hour, and kept the fox curious about that howling thing that chased him so intently and so slowly. The hunters, guided by Rover's bugling voice, would head across lots and surprise the fox as he dodged about looking back over his shoulder at Rover. But the new dog was trained for riding to hounds, and when they set him on a scent he gave one yipe, two barks, a howl

## MY PARENTAL INHERITANCE

and a yelp and was clear over to Witcher's pasture before the Fox Club knew he was gone.

The fox, his tongue hanging out, couldn't keep up the pace, and he holed up in the sandy hill on the back end of our farm. The dog brought up at the hole, his head underground, and the members of the club found his stern sticking up in the air and his tail wagging gaily. His muffled outcry clearly indicated the fox was just ahead of him.

The club prepared to dig out the fox, and members came up to our house to borrow shovels, axes, picks, lanterns, and other implements. They would shove a stick in the hole and feel out its direction, then sink a shaft and feel with the stick again. Then the dog leaped into one of the shafts and started barking. He plunged in beyond his forward shoulders, then stopped and wagged his tail in an ingratiating manner and attempted to back out. One of the hunters became disgusted at such half-hearted attempts on the part of a $75 dog, and presented the dog with a swift kick in his eastern elevation. The effect was marvelous. The dog gave a mufflled yelp and sprang ahead and in an instant was out among the members of the Fox Club holding in his jaws the largest skunk ever seen in captivity. He shook him savagely and the skunk responded nobly. He distributed his favors upon the just and the unjust. Scott covered the situation well when he wrote:

> ". . . and the grim lord of Colonsay
> hath turned him on the ground
> and laughed in death pang that his blade
> the mortal thrust so well repaid."

## MY PARENTAL INHERITANCE

The skunk was dead, but he exacted a fearful retribution. The hunters finally got the skunk away from the dog and threw him down the gully. The dog, however, returned to his hole. If they wanted skunks he knew where they could be found. He brought out another and another. He brought out nine. Each time the hunters felt sure the fox would be next, but the fox was never found, and the dog's nose was never any good again for the fox. Around two in the morning I smelled the hunters bringing back the tools. My father got up and gave them some good suggestions about removing skunk stink from clothing, and they told him to go to hell.

The next morning, directed by something a little stronger than a sense of direction, I rushed to the scene of the massacre and skinned nine skunks which later brought me $1.35. I stretched the skins and nailed them to the shed, and intended to keep my good fortune a secret, but somehow mother got wind of it. She wouldn't let me in the house until I rinsed my hands in vinegar and changed my clothes in the barn. I tried to explain to mother that in time she would get used to it, but I gathered from her remarks that she had no intention of getting used to it. I have observed that women are like that—not waiting to consider that all great enterprises have some slight drawbacks. From that time on she spoke less sincerely of my fitness for the ministry, especially since I bought traps with my $1.35 and subsequently smelled just like the other boys when I went to school.

The farm on which I spent such happy hours was on the easterly slope of Lisbon Ridge, a place my grandfather almost took away from the Indians. I have often wondered why he didn't give it back. It was rocky and rough, and hard to extort

## MY PARENTAL INHERITANCE

a living from. Folks who lived in the more level sections of town said that people on Lisbon Ridge changed work every spring, and one man turned the grindstone while the other ground the noses of his sheep down to a sharp point so they could reach in between rocks and graze. We said, in turn, that their soil was so poor that when they buried anyone in their cemetery they had to put a load of manure in the grave so the soul would rise at the resurrection.

My parents were poor, and my mother was honest. She was an earnest Christian and labored long to plant the good seed in my heart, but this soil was poor too, and she never got a decent crop. My father was a respected citizen but he knew his way around in a cow trade. He wouldn't lie, but at times he was most economical with the truth. Someone would ask him how much milk a cow gave, and he'd say, "Oh, she gives a pail half full." Naturally he would neglect to add that he only milked her once a day, and then in a pail that wouldn't hold a quart.

I was introduced to work very early in life, but not at my request. But father thought growing boys should work, and he had ways of inducing me to accept his theory. Our farm produced switches on every acre.

I soon became aware that anyone could raise a crop but it took a good man to sell it at a satisfactory price. I became a salesman at the age of nine, when father sent me to Lewiston, ten miles away by horse and cart, to sell a load of potatoes. Father said to ask a dollar, but if I couldn't get it to drop down to seventy-five cents. I prodded the old mare along, and thought as I came to a brook that she might like a drink. Over the fence some men were working in a brickyard, and

## MY PARENTAL INHERITANCE

I yelled at them to see if they wanted to buy some potatoes. They said they did. The price of a dollar a bushel was all right, and I drove the mare back home with an empty cart. Father commended my business ability and awakened my interest somewhat in selling.

Life on the old farm developed qualities of frugality, industry, and fortitude. Without these qualities our family would all have starved to death. I didn't die. None of our family died under eighty. The tough ones lived to 105. We raised just about everything we consumed, and manufactured nearly everything we used. It was not, perhaps, the ideal way to live, or to bring up a family—but we made out, and I suppose in our own terms we were happy. We saw little money, and it was not for frivolous use. The marketing was done as much as possible by barter, and it was a sort of Yankee bartering that undoubtedly had a huge influence on many a trade I executed later in life. I have since done business with many a man who reminded me of father—but truth to tell few of them were as good at a dicker.

I told a group of men once that father raised a family of eight children, and never spent $50 a year at grocery stores. One man scoffed, said that soap alone would cost more than that. Father never spent a dollar for soap that I can remember—we made it. I could make some now, if you could stand the smell. All year long we saved our grease: the skimmings from the soup, the boiled dinner, any scraps of salt pork, and the waste from the slaughter of animals. All the wood ashes were kept, too. In March, when the winter broke up and we had a heavy rain, we'd catch a lot of rain water, and then I used to set up the leach. A leach board was kept from the

## MY PARENTAL INHERITANCE

previous years—a groove around the outlines of two barrels and they both drained into one channel.

I would bore a hole in the bottom of each of two barrels and plug them with two sled stakes. Straw went into the bottom of the barrels, with some bricks nearby to keep the holes from plugging up. Then dump in the ashes and wet them down. The ashes would sink and I'd fill the barrels again, add more water, and keep on until the ashes were ready to use. The water and ashes soaked for two days, and then I pulled out the sled stakes and the lye would begin to trickle off the leach board. Mother would then take over.

She got a fire going under the old arch kettle, and dumped in the lye. When the lye was boiling, in would go the year's accumulation of grease and now you had better all stand away back because this is going to stink. It has been sixty years since I smelled it, but it comes back to me across the years as if it were this morning. Of all the unearthly, inhuman, disgusting smells I ever smelled, our homemade soap was the worst by many notches.

Finally the mess would be poured into the soap barrel, and more lye added until the soap would *come*. It would harden into a jelly of a yellowish brown color. It would remove dirt. It would also remove the skin clear up to your elbows in time. But not mine. I didn't use very much, and occasionally mother or grandmother would catch me and give me a scrubbing and rave about why I didn't wash my neck. I continued healthy and hearty, however, and believe it was due to using a minimum of that soap.

Brooms, too—we made our own brooms at times. In those days, brooms sold for twenty-five to thirty-five cents. The last

## MY PARENTAL INHERITANCE

was for a very ornate affair, borne aloft on a tin-peddler's cart. It was like the far-famed willapus-wallapus that had "nineteen white stripes around its tail, each separate stripe being of an entirely different color." Whoever painted broomhandles then had an eye for color and lots of paint.

Aunt Eunice was one who refused to bow the knee to Baal, or to pay such an extortionate price for a broom. I would be nominated to go out in the woods and get some hemlock boughs to make a broom.

The hemlock thicket was on the lower side of the sap berth near the sap house. On about a quarter of an acre the beech and yellow birch had been cut to provide fuel, and the young hemlock had come crowding in. They were presuming upstarts to encroach on ground hitherto sacred to the lordly hardwood trees but, like the lesser peoples who creep into our cities, they consolidated their gains and held on.

The hemlocks are a busy people. The young trees remind one of a sturdy housewife. Not a beauty, but a good woman for a living. They have a clean smell, like newly washed clothes. Fir, spruce, pine, and cedar—each has a perfume of its own.

But I like the hemlock perfume best of all. Under their close-knit branches the rabbit dwelt in peace, and here the jumping mouse had his home, from which he made short excursions over the forest floor in amazing kangaroo-like leaps. Here the partridge reared her brood, and here the thrush at evening sang her lonely, lovely song.

I would return with a load of hemlock and then Aunt Eunice would set about her broom making. She would select the feathery branches and bind the stems together with a

## MY PARENTAL INHERITANCE

stout rope yarn, and then saw off the ends square and drive in the sharpened handle, which tightened the bind. Then she would sweep the floor in a triumphant manner and sing:

> "The days are swiftly passing by
> And I, a pilgrim stranger,
> Would not detain them as they fly
> Those days of toil and danger."

The next time father went to town he would buy a broom, and the hemlock broom would be degraded to the task of sweeping out the shed, but Aunt Eunice was satisfied. She had once more demonstrated to herself that she was no man's slave. If broom makers would charge such outrageous prices, she could rise superior to them and make her own brooms.

I presume in these days of vacuum cleaners, most housewives would give her brooms very little praise; but to me they stand for the old pioneer spirit that faced the wilderness and found a way to get what was needed, or else go without it. The same spirit that is licking the coal strike today. I believe we have a lot of it left and every little while I see something that makes me sure of it.

I can remember, too, the warming days of spring when the wool was clipped from the old sheep, washed and hung on the barnyard fence to dry. Later the womenfolks would go up into the open attic and spin. We dried apples and packed mincemeat. We picked our own caraway seed, and put up salt cucumbers, and put down our own pork and smoked our own hams. We raised what we ate, or ate what we raised—depending on the crops, the weather, and our own ability to provide. We took farm products to market, cut wood for our-

## MY PARENTAL INHERITANCE

selves and sold enough to pay for flour and molasses. Mother set bread every night, and varied the diet with corn bread or brown bread. Eggs and milk and butter and cheese were available up to the limit of our production—and backward as those days were I have seen times since when the custard pies were scarcer.

I was sixteen when I broke the home ties. I was strong, knew how to work, and had a boy's ambition to make my own way. I was in favor of the prospect in Massachusetts, where higher wages rewarded less work.

## 8

## MY FIRST STORE

When I took over the store at Harmony I figured the stock was a detriment, and my chief asset was the location. Harmony is still a one-horse town as towns are graded by city people, and sits 18 miles from any other sizeable community at the head of a branch line of the Maine Central Railroad. All the surrounding towns had to come to Harmony to do business, and my store was a potential trading center for a huge territory. A large creamery, corn-packing plant, and a small wool processing mill were our industries, but the railroad did a big business with lumber, pulp wood, cattle, hay, and other farm and forest products.

The previous owner thought he had milked the cow and would sell her before she went dry. He had the usual country store stock—boots and shoes, dry goods, hardware and groceries all jumbled together. One window was boarded up, but the other had an unseasonal display—it was March—of a fly trap, some bats, a catcher's mask, a pair of nose baskets, and a croquet set. This was typical of my prede-

## MY FIRST STORE

cessor's methods of merchandising. I had bought the stock at inventory and there was $2,000 worth of it at cost, but a lot of it looked to me like a poor investment.

I began business in the Harmony store by washing the floor, for which I got the dirtiest water I ever saw. Three times over still produced dirty water, but I thought that was enough for the first day. You can appreciate how destitute the store stock was when I say that we hadn't any cheese. I told my clerk that I'd set a dozen mouse traps if I had some cheese. He said, "Sometimes mice run along the walls, and you can catch them without bait." We set the twelve traps, and next morning we had twelve mice. We caught mice without bait for weeks, but never got twelve at once again.

The principal display in the old store was a case of tobacco, a display no customer could help seeing. Of course, tobacco is one thing a store doesn't have to display—anyone who smokes, chews, or takes snuff is bound to remember to get his supply. So I put the tobacco down under the counter and saved the show case for something that needed displaying. I was trying to make up my mind when a drummer came in. He had the answer: "Hang four doors to cover those shelves and use that show case and I'll put you in a stock of $800 worth of hardware, and if it doesn't turn in 60 days I'll take it back."

I said, "The place is yours, but don't be surprised to see it coming back." He said that for years and years I sold more hardware than any other country store on his list, but before I came he had been trying to get a stock in without convincing the previous owner.

As my drummer was figuring out the hardware list, a little old man of sixty or so came in and looked about. He acted as

# MY FIRST STORE

if he had made a mistake, and inquired for the former owner. I said I was the new owner, and we talked about a few prices for a minute or two. Then he asked me what I was paying for eggs, and would I take what he had. I didn't know what I was getting into—he had come down over the muddy roads from a neighboring town, and had brought all the eggs in that town with him. We packed eggs and put up goods the rest of the afternoon.

His purchases came to $60 more than the eggs, and the goods were for all the people who had sent eggs down by him. He settled up, and then said, "Oh, I forgot—take out a peck of oats for my horses." I wrote out an order on the mill for some oats and wouldn't take his money. I said, "Come back when you get the horses fed." Meantime I opened a can of sardines, got out some crackers, a few cookies, a banana, and a bottle of tonic. I gave him this lunch when he came back, and said, "I wouldn't think of letting you start the long trip home without something to eat."

The old fellow seemed in a daze, but he chewed up the lunch and thanked me endlessly, climbed on his wagon and drove home. I found out afterwards that he went to every house in town before he got into bed, and told people that the new trader was a good fellow. I don't think anyone else got a cent out of that town as long as I was in business.

Similarly, a young farmer came in and bought a big order. I asked, "Have you got any children?" He said, "Three." So I went among my stock and bought out a pail of clove drops. They had summered, and the heat had stuck them all together. I hit the pail with the back of an axe, and put about a pound in each of three bags, which I gave to the customer

## MY FIRST STORE

for his children. Afterwards I put up the rest of the pail in small bags and kept them for favors.

Later my young farmer came in laughing. He said his wife took the little girl over to Athens to trade, and the storekeeper didn't give her anything. "So she got up in my lap when she got home and made me promise never to shop in Athens again." I couldn't afford to give candy to every customer with children, but the little girl never had cause to bemoan the lack of generosity at my place.

I began my Harmony career with a mix-up that perhaps tokened the style of my business. I didn't take up my option on the place until after the first of April, so the taxes still had to be paid by the former owner. He was so mad he nearly burst when he realized what I'd done, but to my thinking that was just a ramification of the sale and I forgot about it. He told me he'd like to remain in the house for the time being, as he wanted to clean up some business. That suited me, and I simply took one room until he was ready to move. I paid for the stock and paid $1,000 on the real estate. He was to take a mortgage for the balance. Along about August he told me he was ready to make the deed, and he insisted on dating it back to April. Meantime, he had sold a big pile of manure around the barn, and although I saw it being carted away I didn't think much about it at the time.

But when the deed was finally passed, in August, I put in a bill for four months rent on the house at $10 a month, and a bill for $25 for the manure. Manure goes with the land in real estate deals, and since the place was now mine as of April 1, I was entitled to it. I was also entitled to rent. He roared like a lion, but he had no way out. He always claimed I was a crook.

## MY FIRST STORE

This took my mind off some of the details of the first few months of business and was no doubt a nice bit of priming, but I really suffered with one early experience. I had to buy a carload of seed oats almost the day I took over. I telephoned to a broker and asked if he had a car nearby. He said he had, and I asked for the price, which he gave. It was higher than I expected to pay and I balked, but he said they were extra fine and nearby and I could expect them in a week, so I finally bought.

This fellow was probably the biggest liar in the State of Maine, and that's a liar's territory. The oats were in the elevator in Chicago, and they were sulphured oats. Weather-stained oats are bleached with sulphur to make them look better. This usually kills the germ, and they are not fit for seed. When the car finally came men were standing around waiting for seed, their ground ready, and we put out 500 bushels in a very few minutes.

I found a card tacked up in the car and it said, "This car contains sulphured oats and they have been sold as such by the shipper." I was so green I didn't know what it meant, although I remember I did put a handful in a box of earth to test the sprout. In about a week the farmers began to come in with their sad story—no sprouts. I was in despair, but I knew my whole future depended on how I acted, so I took the bull by the horns. I paid every man back what he gave me for oats, and notified the broker. He came back very savagely with a story that they never guaranteed seed oats, and demanded pay. I had my mad up, and I told him that he knew very well sulphured oats were not seed oats, and that I wouldn't pay for what we had sowed and lost. The next thing

## MY FIRST STORE

I got was a letter from an attorney, and I picked up my evidence and went to call on him.

I laid my cards on the table and said, "If you think this is a good case go ahead and sue, but remember—all you'll get is what a Somerset County jury will give you, and maybe some of them have been swindled with poor seed."

He nodded, and took me over to the office of the firm, and we soon made an agreement. I was to pay for the balance of the car, but they were to discount the five hundred bushels I had refunded on. As it turned out, the adventure was good advertising for me, but it scared me to have to stand up and fight a big firm the first thing. It did give me a lot of confidence, and I saw that sometimes a man has to fight to get what belongs to him.

Anyway, I went my merry way getting acquainted with business opportunities in Harmony, and when January 1 came around I took inventory. I went through my books and discounted drastically any doubtful bill. I had done a business of $30,000. I had repaired and painted the house and had put in a pumping plant and a new bathroom. I had disposed of old stock at a sacrifice and was afraid I had made a poor showing. When the inventory was done, and my clerks had gone home, I put the figures together. They showed a profit of $2,964.18—without counting the increased value of my real estate. I was sure there was an error. I checked back over my figures until my head swam. The only error I found was a stock of paint that had been overlooked, valued at $150. I threw that in for good measure and faced the new year with courage enough to tackle anyone or anything.

## 9

## PRUNES FOR SAWMILLS

---

AFTER the Harmony business seemed to be under way with good prospects, I knew that I hadn't made a mistake, and I really went after business. I tried to recall all the little things I remembered from my days in Portsmouth, and whenever opportunity gave occasion I'd think up some new stunts of my own. I lamented frequently that my show windows weren't adequate, but the Independent Order of Odd Fellows, my landlords, couldn't seem to recognize my need. I was just about to send in my name and see if I couldn't take up the matter under the order of business when they came around and told me my rent was to go up.

I couldn't really complain about the rise in rent, for my business warranted more than I had been paying—but I pointed scornfully at the show windows and the committee that called on me nodded. The windows went in and my rent went up. I filled one of the windows with the new hardware stock, and put on my thinking cap to make use of the other. The previous season had been a failure for apples,

## PRUNES FOR SAWMILLS

and I thought to myself, "I'd even put in a display of Ben Davis apples if I could get them," Ben Davis being the meanest apple ever invented. I was thinking how lovely it would make my competitors feel if I could fill that big window with any kind of apple at all.

Then a drummer came in with a bargain on prunes. Prunes—apples? Why not? The prunes I had in stock were 50/60 count and cost twelve cents a pound. He offered me a 90/100 count and four and one-half cents a pound in 25-pound boxes. I tried for a better price, and he offered me a ton at four cents. I finally got half a ton at three and three-quarters cents, and I dumped the window full of them when they came. On the glass I painted, "7¢ a pound, $1.39 a box." I retired to the rear of the store to await the community's decision; would prunes sell when apples were scarce?

In a scant few minutes a rough, tough, and nasty looking man came in and gruffly asked, "What's the matter with them prunes?" I explained that their quality was as good as the best, but the size was small. He took a box to try them. Next day he came in and bought ten boxes. Not knowing the gentleman, I couldn't imagine what he planned to do with ten boxes of prunes, so I made discreet inquiry and found he operated a sawmill about ten miles back in the woods and had a big crew of men at work. Prunes solved a dietary problem for him, and for this service on my part he was disposed to trade with me for other items. In a few weeks he was paying me between fifty and a hundred dollars a week. It struck me that sawmill operators represented a place to expand business.

I located 19 mills in various parts of my territory, and I

## PRUNES FOR SAWMILLS

would look for bargains. The problem of feeding a crew of men deep in the woods is one of huge proportions, and it pleased these men to find a storekeeper who catered to their remote trade. I got a duplicating machine and mailed them all a card when I had something good. The day after all the sawmill men in the region would come in and practically buy me out. I took the drummers in on my scheme, and I insisted on some bargain for my woods trade every trip. Doing business with housewives is one aspect of the grocery trade, but being a purchasing agent for the rawboned appetites of Maine lumberjacks is a specialty I always liked.

Besides that, going out so far for business gave me other ideas. I saw that the smart storekeeper must buy what his own particular customers need—merely carrying standard items isn't enough. I found, too, that the smart storekeeper may have to introduce some commodities his customers have never seen before.

It was that way with flour. I knew that Maine is a cream-of-tartar biscuit state, and a good flour is necessary for good cream-of-tartar biscuits. I wanted a high-grade, winter-wheat patent, particularly because the feed that one buys with his flour is an item of consideration, and Maine farmers prefer a soft wheat middling or bran. I finally located a firm that could supply my wants and would extend credit, so I ordered a carload of flour and feed. And I immediately found out that something besides a counter and cash register is needed if a man is going to make money running a store.

My first barrel of flour went to a man whose wife used a barrel every three weeks. In a few hours the man came in with a sorry-looking biscuit and said, "My wife can't use it;

## PRUNES FOR SAWMILLS

she is used to a good flour." I knew the real trouble lay in one truth I couldn't explain—the woman had never used a good flour before. A patent flour contains a lot of gluten and it expands in baking, while a lower grade is largely starch and doesn't expand—and so takes more flour per batch of biscuits. She had simply used too much flour. I have known merchants who would have explained this to the rage of a man who knew he had married a good cook—but not me.

I said, "I'll send and get the flour, and give you your money back, but before I do, I want you to try a batch my way. Tell your wife to use three-quarters as much flour as before, and leave the dough so soft she'll have to pick it off the board with a knife."

In about an hour he came back to the store with another biscuit. It was a beauty. He grinned and said, "My wife says she guesses she never had any good flour before." I made it a point to teach the women of Harmony how to use good flour, and my sales went up. I had a good agency, and was able to sell a high grade flour in a territory that never before could handle it. Counting my feed end of the business, I was doing wonders simply because I knew how to make biscuits.

Flour gave me a number of headaches, but I think I usually came out on top. Just before World War I, I was hanging off on my usual order. The millers would put out a lot of propaganda every year about the short wheat crop, or how it was sprouting in the stack if there were a big crop, and they probably fooled a lot of storekeepers every year. But I trusted my flour salesman, and he usually held up my interests. One night in August he called me up and said, "Have you bought your flour?"

## PRUNES FOR SAWMILLS

"No, you're too high."

He adopted a confidential tone over long distance and whispered, "My firm heard some news today that made them buy 5,000 barrels, and I can let you in on the same price." The whispering seemed valid, and I said, "OK, I'll take five cars, 100 barrels to the car and fill up with feed. Ship the first car anytime, and follow the others every 60 days."

The next night the World War broke out and wheat and flour started up. I moved my price along with the prevailing market, and kept fairly happy. Along in the next winter I read in the Lewiston *Journal* that something was going to be done to restrict the sale of flour, and it seemed to me the place to start would be to forbid the sale of barrels. I had over a hundred barrels in the store, and I put on my hat and went right out in the street. I stopped everyone who came along and whispered, "How's your flour? Would you like to buy five barrels?"

Most of them looked at me curiously and asked, "What do you know?" I said, "Nothing, but I guess you'll find flour a good thing to have." I sold my last barrel before the order came restricting sales to one-eighth barrel sacks and making it necessary to buy an equal amount of cereal. My store was a happy place for the next few days—my customers were happy because they had the flour, and I was happy because I had the money. I raised hell on feeds during this time. I bought feeds as low as $31.50 a ton, and by the time it arrived on my spur track the price was up to $83. I'd sell out at $65 a ton and everyone loved me.

The business I had built up with the lumbermen began to make a different kind of a return. After the long lumber was

## PRUNES FOR SAWMILLS

cut off, the pulp wood operations would come, and they are financed a little differently. A man would come in for a few groceries and explain that he had no money, but he had a contract to put 500 cords of pulp on the bog. I'd ask, "How are you going to be paid?"

He would say something like this: "A dollar when peeled, a dollar piled, a dollar on the landing, and the rest in May."

I'd ask, "Haven't got any horses to buy, old doctor bills, or taxes out of this?" If he said no, I'd tell him to order what he needed, and pay me as fast as he got his money.

A lot of his payments for peeling and piling would go for labor, but I'd keep giving him credit, and in May he would come in with a check for, say, $750. He owed me at least $250 by then, and it broke up my whole financial structure when I had to cash his check to get my money. But I rigged another scheme, and have prospered under it ever since.

There was no bank very near and few men had a bank account. I'd give him about $25 in cash, and then make him out a flock of checks: $10, $20, and a few $50—none larger. When he wanted some money he'd cash one of my checks, but sometimes he'd go over a year before he cashed them all. Sometimes the men he cashed them with would hold them, and occasionally it was a couple of years before my checks got back to the bank.

One day my banker said, "You have a nice account here. In fact, you carry a balance of over $3,000 all the time—but one thing we can't understand, some of your checks are a year or two old." I explained, and he said, "Fine, fine—splendid." I asked, "How about using this balance when I have a heavy draft coming in?" He said, "Go ahead, and we'll see you through."

The upshot of this was that I borrowed very little money from banks after that, but did business with money put up by my pulp-wood operators. I used to smile when they'd come in and thank me for helping them out! Just what this backlog of funds meant to me is hard to recall. I expanded in any line that seemed a likely prospect, and was able to see it through without stinting the rest of my business.

Hardly a week went by but some occasion to turn over a piece of change came to hand, and I would have been unable to proceed without my understanding with the bank. I don't recall that my credit to the pulp men was ever a total loss, and I suppose in addition to enlarging my business at the time, I financed the long trains of pulp wood that the Maine Central hauled down from Harmony. Naturally, too, my bank was doing business with my deposits—and it is doubtful if such a small amount of money ever did so much elsewhere.

One fine-appearing man once got me for $100, and I found he owed everyone and I couldn't get a cent. I wanted a mortgage on his cattle, but a mortgage for an old bill can be upset by a bankruptcy. But a mortgage to secure a new debt will hold, so I had to create a new debt. I told my man, "Why don't you borrow the money to pay my bill? Joe Martin will lend you the money." I tipped Joe off, and he lent the money and my bill was paid. Joe took a mortgage on the stock, and then assigned it to me.

I really had good luck on most of my credit transactions, mostly because I kept my eyes open both before and after the account was opened. In a short time I began to act as

## PRUNES FOR SAWMILLS

credit reference for my territory. I imagine there were plenty of smiles in Dun's office when my reports went in, but I put down the things I felt to be true and was reasonably successful at it. I got an inquiry once about a man in town, and I wrote in, "His disposition to cheat people is good, but I don't believe anyone is fool enough to trust him."

In less than three months this man went into bankruptcy, and not for any trifling amount, either. The Dun's man came around and I was apologetic. "Sorry I slipped up on that man," I said. "I should have given a more businesslike rating."

Dun's man said, "We sent a copy of your report to all our customers, and after that none of our customers was fool enough to trust him—none of them lost a cent. Your credit ratings are in terms that mean something when figures don't."

Another bankruptcy that I remember was a man who traded with me some, not a large account, but he seemed all right. He owed all hands when he finally gave up, and I wasn't particularly upset over it. The wife of my competitor gave the poor devil a good hiding in the street, and I felt sorry for him. When I got him alone I told him to come in and get $25 worth of credit until he could get on his feet again. Part of what he owed me was for seed oats, and he had planted a big acreage. He cried when I told him he could have credit and said, "You won't lose by this."

In the fall he poked his head in the front door and said, "Leave the mill door unlocked tonight," and was gone. In the morning I found 100 bushels of oats on the mill floor, which paid his account with interest and possibly puzzled his bankruptcy auditor.

I don't know how many farmers have tried to hoodwink

me by leaving things in a bag. A man came in with two bushels of dried beans one day, and I said I'd take them on his account. He said, "I've set the bag by the scales. Weigh them and give me credit." Just as I suspected, he had threshed them on the barn floor, and when he gathered them up he had a generous sprinkling of everything.

I went to the account register and wrote out a slip, "Credit, by two bushels of hen dung, 35¢." The next time he settled up he howled like a dog baying at the moon. "Now, now," I said, "I'll just call your attention to the Pure Food Law, which stipulates that all food must bear the name of its principal ingredients." The threat of prosecution under the law didn't scare him, of course, but he had to admit my allowance was generous under the circumstances.

We bought eggs in unlimited quantities. From July on we had to be careful. Farmers were busy with haying, and the hens weren't watched so closely. One would steal away a nest and set on the eggs a week or so. Of course, the eggs would go in the crate just the same, and once a lot got by the clerk and caused trouble. The next time the farmer came in the clerk said, "Mr. Crymble, those last eggs you brought in were rotten." The old farmer struck an attitude of surprise and said, "Well—damn a hen that will lay rotten eggs!"

The worst thing we had to deal with, though, was odd lots of country butter. When Bill Nye was in our part of the country, he saw a farmer driving his cows in a yoke, like oxen, and Bill said, "I wish the farmers would work their cows less and their butter more." Some of the butter was calculated to make an angel weep because he couldn't swear. We had our regular supply throughout the year, and we knew it was good,

## PRUNES FOR SAWMILLS

but we also had some customers who let their cream get ahead of them in June or July and they'd come in to buy some groceries and ask, "Don't you want to buy some good butter?"

Such people sold only a few pounds a year, and if their trade seemed to warrant it, we'd take their butter no matter what it tasted like. After it stayed in the refrigerator a few weeks or months it wasn't improved any, and many a pound of it I've discarded after a reasonable period of incarceration. We worked them off if we could, but sometimes we just plain couldn't.

I remember once a man came in and asked, "Have you any poor butter?" I looked him straight in the eye, and he stared back. I said, with extreme truthfulness, "Yes, sir, I have." He said he'd take a pound, and I wrapped up some butter that almost threw me while I was tying the string. The next night the man came in again, and casually stated, "I'll take two more pounds of that butter."

While I held it down and reached for the wrapping paper I said, "I wish you'd tell me why you want this—I've been ripped up the back plenty of times for selling stuff like this."

He told me the secret. "My wife has two big booby boys by her first husband, and they're visiting us. They'll put a quarter of a pound of butter on a biscuit and swallow it, but by God this butter makes 'em stand back."

Once, only once, an old lady came in and asked if I'd buy a bushel of beechnuts. I asked her what she wanted for them, and she said they ought to be worth a dollar and a half. I gave her the money and sold the beechnuts inside of an hour to a drummer. How anyone could gather a bushel of those little three-cornered nuts and feel repaid with $1.50 is something I'll never know. My notion is she had all the time in the world and no money.

Occasionally I fostered some stunt that stimulated business without necessitating my opening a new line. One fall I listened to sitters in the store relate how their deer got away. I suggested they were all better talkers than shooters, and proposed a shooting match and supper by the losing side. The supper was to be at Grange Hall on Thanksgiving day. The idea stimulated the sale of guns and ammunition, and we had a grand time. We each had three shots at a standing target at 100 yards, no rest. I got a 200-yard target and made a backboard four feet square. Most of the hunters couldn't even hit the backboard. The bull's-eye on a 200-yard target is as big as a dinner plate, but no one hit it. I had a little 30-30 carbine and three of us on my side used it. The three best shots were made with my rifle. I sold 30-30 carbines all fall, got a good supper out of it, built up considerable good will—but noticed that the number of deer shot didn't increase any.

My thoughts went back to the old farm when a man came in one day to sell me a big hog. "How big?" He said, "Real big." I said, "An old stag?" He said, "Yes." And I told him to keep him. An old stag is simply a boar that has been kept to two or three years before he is reformed, and after that he talks about what a fellow he was before his operation. He grows fat and lazy and looks like a million dollars to those who never met one. The salt pork is bomb-proof. I've seen a man lay a piece on the block and hit it with the cleaver and nearly get his brains knocked out by the rebound. Nothing but a fair price would make me buy an old stag, and as pork

## PRUNES FOR SAWMILLS

was worth twelve cents a pound I offered this man five cents and listened to him rave. He tried all the other places and finally brought him in.

We got rid of the hams and shoulders by slicing them up, but the loins were our real problem. One chop would feed an ordinary family a week, but we finally wore him out. We put the salt pork down cellar and awaited a victim. We expected some lumber camp would buy it, because they use it in beans, and after 24 hours' baking it softens up a little. But one day I came back from a trip and the clerk told me he'd sold the barrel of pork. An old farmer who didn't like the prices dealers offered him for some worn-out dairy cows hit on the idea of peddling them around. He wanted a little pork to go with his beef. He asked no questions and the clerk didn't prompt him. The clerk told him the price was about a cent over common pork, and he took it. I never heard from it, and never asked.

Once in a while I'd buy some bull beef, which is not choice fare. It has a bad reputation, mainly because people try to fry it and it doesn't fry worth a cent. Once a farmer came in and said he had a nice Holstein bull, and I said I didn't want him. He said, "Now this bull isn't going to be tough—he's thoroughbred, and he's been kept fat ever since he was a calf, and he's nice."

I said, "Now look, for your own sake, don't tell that to anyone else. What you should say is, he's been poor all his life and was fatted up in the last three months. Then the tissue would be nearly all new and possibly tender—but you've probably got the toughest bull in captivity."

Of course, he said I was crazy, and he went down to Skow-

## PRUNES FOR SAWMILLS

hegan and sold the bull to someone else. He came back later and said, "You were right, I sold him, and took home a big sirloin roast. My wife cooked it two days and couldn't stick a fork in the gravy."

Occasionally, however, I'd buy some bull beef, and try to sell it to people who knew how to cook it. The secret is easy. I'd frequently cook a piece at home, and it was always good. I'd bring some water to a boil, put in about a half cup of salt, and plunge about ten pounds of bull brisket into the water. The boiling water would sear the meat and keep the juices in. I'd fill up the stove and let it boil until the wood burned out. Next time I was in the kitchen I'd fill up the stove again, and leave the kettle tightly covered and boiling for the most of three days.

When I could lift the bones out of the meat I'd leave the meat to cool in the liquor. The kettle was a mass of jelly in the morning, because bull beef is full of gelatine. No one could ask for a better tasting meat, and it was tender and appetizing. Once in a while my wife would cook a piece of cow beef the same way, but the female of the species won't stand under such treatment. If I was sure the customer would cook it my way, I'd sell him some bull beef and wait for his praise. Otherwise, it is a sure way to alienate good will.

Buying odd items is tricky business. My predecessor in the store got split wide open on one occasion. There was an old timer in Wellington who made beautiful axe handles. They were shaved by hand from straight-grained rock maple, and were in great demand by wood choppers. These handles retailed for thirty-five cents, and the old timer sold them to retailers at twenty-five cents each by the dozen. One time my

## PRUNES FOR SAWMILLS

predecessor didn't treat the old fellow right and offered him fifteen cents each. The old man tried to get more and felt pretty much let down. Finally the old man said, "Well, I s'pose I've got to take it," and he went home. In a few days he brought in three dozen handles—white and smooth and beautiful. The storekeeper paid for them, and the old man went home.

The first customer raised an awful yell. The handles were made of basswood—a lovely soft white wood that works easily, but is absolutely worthless for an axe handle. The old man never came back, and it wasn't until I bought the store that he came in and let me do business with him at the old price.

## 10

## POTATOES

MY EXPERIENCE with the pulp wood men opened my eyes in a direction that few country storekeepers have ever looked. That is, a store can sell only as much as the customers can pay for; so before the business can expand much the storekeeper must look up ways for his customers to get money. It's as broad as it's long.

I started buying produce. I found outlets for cord wood, pulp, lumber, berries, hides, cattle, hogs, and anything my territory had to sell. Yellow-eyed beans were as staple as sugar, and we took all they'd bring in. Potatoes were handled by many buyers, and I paid off for several of them. All this brought folks into my store to collect their money, and if they happened to owe me a bill I naturally took it out. But now I began handling such items mainly because it helped my customers toward a better life—and what was good for business was good for me.

Many amusing things happened. One day a man who owed me $100 came in and said, "Gould, the only way I can pay

## POTATOES

you is to sell my potatoes, and they're only worth twenty-eight cents today."

I said, "Don't sell. Give me your note for three months, and if they haven't started up by then, they won't anyway." When the note came due potatoes were worth eighty cents, and the man paid me. He was pleased and thanked me clear out to the door. The next fall he came in and said, "Gould, make out another note for what I owe you," and I said, "No, sir!" He said, "Why not? You did last fall." I had to explain that whereas potatoes were twenty-eight cents a year ago, they were now a dollar. He said, "Yes, but they're going to $1.50 sure."

I said, "Don't ever gamble on potatoes at $1. You better sell enough to pay me, and if you're smart you'll sell them all." He sold some and paid me, and held the rest of them for a rise that never came. In April he shuffled in and collected fifty-eight cents a bushel for what he had left. He said, "I wish I'd owed you more last fall." Doing business with farmers is often like that; they work hard, but they often miss a good market by an incurable optimism that keeps them hanging on for a better price.

But a man who does business with a farmer must keep a sharp eye and a quick mind, or he'll get some unpleasant surprises. The honest farmer will bear more watching than most storekeepers have time for. One farmer tried to sell me potatoes, and I offered him a dollar a bushel for a hundred bushels. We dickered for two months, and I thought if he wanted a good old-fashioned kind of trade I could accommodate him. At the end of two months I dropped my price to eighty cents. He whined, but taxes were due and I suspected

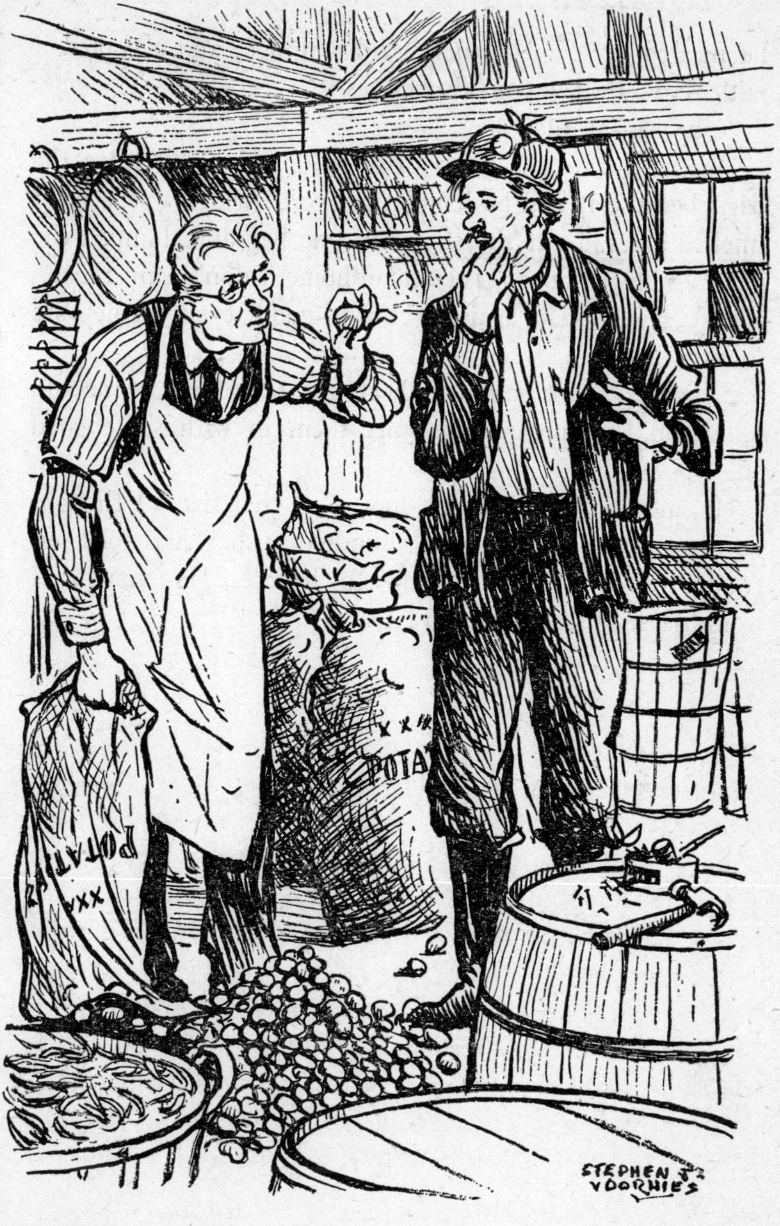
XXX
POTAT
STEPHEN VOORHIES

## POTATOES

he needed to sell. He finally said as much, and accepted. I said, "Now these are good potatoes?"

"Oh, yes—all nice ones."

When he brought them in he said, "Now I'll leave the bags, because it will be handier for you," which was when I smelled a rat. I cut the string on one bag and dumped the potatoes on the floor. "Take them home, I don't want them," I said. He whined again, "They're good, even if they are small."

I said, "I'm not going to cheat you, take them home and sell them to someone else—mix them in with some good ones."

He said, "I guess I've got enough of that size." I thought he must have—we racked the hundred bushels and took out twenty-five bushels too small to handle. He thought I wouldn't see them until too late.

## 11

## CREDIT, GOING AND COMING

THE real problem of storekeeping is credit—getting credit from banks and wholesale houses, and giving credit to customers. I'd be hard put to suggest which direction is the more important. If he can't get credit, the storekeeper could never operate; and if he doesn't extend credit he could never do the kind of business I have done. Both directions have difficulties—to pay the wholesalers in order to keep the credit good; and to collect accounts in order to live. I have sweat copiously in both areas, and have come to the conclusion that credit is one whole problem, and it all involves constant care. No matter which direction I went, it still had to do with money.

After I bought at Harmony I had easy credit for a short time on the goods I was pushing. Flour and food credit was generous, and I often found a car on my track in the morning and had to wait to find out how much it cost. I'd get word the brokers had it running and didn't want to pay demurrage, "so put it in the warehouse and pay when you want to." But when the war came along the authorities tightened up, and

## CREDIT, GOING AND COMING

I got word all bills had to be paid in 30 days. This, to me, was like being kicked by a horse, and demonstrated immediately the connection between the two kinds of credit. I started a collection campaign among my customers and soon had the money, but it put a scare into me for a while.

I had a fair supply of working capital when I bought, but it soon vanished like dew before the sun, and I had nothing to pay bills with except accounts. Country storekeeping depends on such a variety of collection methods that it is almost suicide to adopt a uniform policy. I tried to collect and limit credit to those who would pay in 30 days—but I had to make exceptions nearly every day. Most of the farmers did business with the creamery, and their checks would come in once a month—giving me quite a roll on payday. Of course, in the long run I either collected everything or allowed for it one way or another—but I couldn't put my customers on the same schedule the wholesalers adopted with me.

The hardware company surprised me by shipping $800 worth of new stock on 60 days' time with very few inquiries. I had always had a bank account, and had borrowed money before—paying it back on time—so I wasn't too bad a reference, but it was not a business reference. It did surprise me how easily I got credit—but it also surprised me to find out how hard it was to keep this credit good. My customers would buy a bill of goods and promise to pay it in 30 days, and if they paid in a year they thought I ought to give them a cigar.

I remember one of these thirty-day fellows. He assured me he could pay—maybe before. I let him have $25 worth of goods, and "long time I no see him." He calmly ignored state-

## CREDIT, GOING AND COMING

ments and letters, until I penned him one of my own particular brand of letters. I wrote:

DEAR SIR:

When you asked for credit you promised to pay me in 30 days. You assured me you could do this, if not sooner. Now nine months have passed and I have never seen you or heard from you. I realize you may be hard up. I know what it is to be hard up, and have been as hard up as anyone in the past—but when I owed a bill and couldn't pay it as I agreed, I always wrote my creditor and explained the situation and told him just what I could do and I never had any trouble. Now you don't answer my letters and your promises are no good. I am going to make you a promise. If I don't hear from you by next Saturday I will sue you on Monday, and if you don't believe I keep my promises, just wait until Monday.

Yours truly,<br>R. E. GOULD.

On Saturday a young lady came in and handed me a letter. It contained four pages of abuse, but it had $25 in it. I receipted the bill and called it that. I had lost a customer, but got my money. The next Thursday, however, in came the man and warmed his hands at the stove. I thought, "He'll wait till I see him, and then go and trade with my competitor to make me feel bad." So I sneaked out of the back door to deprive him of some satisfaction. At one o'clock I came back in time to see him loading a tremendous order of groceries in his wagon—and my clerk was helping him! He had bought

## CREDIT, GOING AND COMING

about $40 worth, and paid cash. I couldn't figure it out for a while, but the truth was he owed every storekeeper in town but me. He couldn't let them see him with money—but I didn't count anymore.

Credit is sometimes hard to figure out, but I have always observed that honest intentions are the second best thing to honest actions. The former owner had a line of rubber footwear that was valuable. He had some stock, and advised me to keep the line. In August the salesman came in and asked for the former owner. I introduced myself, and the drummer gave me a long icy stare. Then he said, "I might as well be plain with you. It is doubtful if my house will approve your credit right away. But I advise you to keep the line even if it's on C.O.D., and if you handle the goods well they may give you credit later."

I placed my order, but was surprised that the goods came with a bill that wasn't due until December. When the first of December came around I was stuck—we hadn't had any snow, and I hadn't sold ten dollars' worth of the stock. I scraped up $50 and sent it in along with a letter that explained how I stood—stock on my shelves, no snow, no prospect of sales until the winter really struck.

I got the nicest letter I ever saw from them, saying they were glad I'd written, that they would gladly extend the time 30 days, and if that wasn't enough to write them again. It was enough, and I cleaned them up and thanked them. When the drummer came the next August I said, "You told me your house was tough on credit, but they are extremely nice."

He said, "Mr. Gould, you wrote them on the date the bill

## CREDIT, GOING AND COMING

was due—that's all they want. Our credit men will approve all the credit you want from now on—but if you hadn't written him you'd now be C.O.D. along with a lot of others."

One time I went to New York to see what would come to my net, and I was on lower Broadway where the wholesale dry goods center then was. I saw some bait in a window and went in. I told the young man who I was and that I was interested in some hose in the window. He asked, "How many can you use?" I told him ten dozen or so. And he asked, "Have you ever seen our Mr. Smith?" I said I hadn't had the pleasure, so he called another man whose name may possibly have been Smith. Mr. Smith asked a few questions and went back in his office. Pretty soon he gave the clerk the high sign, and in a matter of minutes I had bought $800 worth of goods. The clerk asked, "When will you be home?" I said in two days, and he told me, "These goods will be there when you get back."

When I got through with the clerk I went into the office and gaffled Mr. Smith. "Tell me," I said, "how in hell you judge credit. You never saw me before, never heard of me. You looked me up in Dun's and if I am rated you ship $800 worth of goods and never turn a hair."

Mr. Smith spread his hands as if the answer were kindergarten stuff. "You come from Maine," he said. "Maine, New Hampshire, Vermont—you don't come here very much. You don't buy much when you come. But if you can't pay when the bill is due—you worry about it, don't you?"

I said, "Of course."

"Well," he came back, "one man is enough to worry. If

## CREDIT, GOING AND COMING

you came from Alabama and owed us $50,000 and couldn't pay you wouldn't worry a damned bit. We would have to worry. One is enough."

I have often wondered how a Jew on lower Broadway knew me so well. I've done more worrying about money I owe than I have about money due me. Once when I was feeling poor I got out some invoices and found I owed my chief wholesale grocer over $1,200—some of it three months old. I got up the next morning and went into Portland and saw the credit man. I showed him the invoices and said, "I am going to stop buying of you, and everytime your man comes I am going to give him all the money I can, until I reduce this amount by half."

He laughed at me, "I'd like the money all right, but don't you stop buying from us. We know who you are and what you're doing. Keep it up. Your credit is good here. Go ahead and buy all you can sell. It doesn't do us any good to sink money in an old-timer, but when we see a young man on the way up we stand behind him."

I have been helped tremendously by credit men and banks, and they deserve all manner of praise. They have a hard row to hoe—I suppose it's worse than keeping a store; but without them I'd have stopped long ago. High finance is pretty far removed from the rural grocery counter, but somehow I figured out some of it when I was young and I've had my share of business on other people's money.

But I've always had to give a thought to the folks who try to do business on my money—a practice of which I highly disapprove. You see, the credit man for a big wholesale house

## CREDIT, GOING AND COMING

has certain business guides to help him. But the storekeeper looks a man in the eye and has to make up his mind immediately whether his credit is good, how good, or not. Like most storekeepers, if the sum at stake were a dollar or so, I'd let it go and figure I was well rid of a bad one before he got enough to ruin me. But when the prospect was good for a large order, I'd look him over carefully.

One day a man came in and greeted me with a smile and handshake and said, "My name is Jim Fisher. I've just bought the Frank Benson place. I paid $200 down, and have just sold a farm in Corinna that will pay me $300 a year to take care of this. I've got ten cows in the creamery, a good team, and all the tools I'll need. So I'd like to buy my grain and groceries from you and pay you when I get my check."

I asked him when he put his cream in the creamery, and he said yesterday. Yesterday was payday at the creamery, so it would be some time before I could expect a settlement. I made a hasty guess and said, "I imagine you'll want about $80 credit?" He said about that. I made out to appear willing, but I said, "I hear a lot of these things and I can't remember very well, so I'll just write this down." So I wrote:

> "For the purpose of obtaining credit from R. E. Gould I make the following statement of my resources: I own the Frank Benson Farm in —— of 110 acres; deed in my own name with a mortgage on it for $1,000. I own a team of horses and ten cows and all farm tools, and I also own a mortgage for $2,000 on a farm in Corinna payable $300 a year—all free from incumbrance except as stated."

## CREDIT, GOING AND COMING

I said, "Is that it?" and he said it was. I had him sign it, had it witnessed, put it in the safe, and handed him out the goods. When payday at the creamery came around, he didn't show up. He made no reply to my letters, so after a reasonable time I started suit. He told his neighbors he was going to show me a thing or two, and went to court prepared to take a poor debtor's oath and be free of me. The little bit of paper I had in my safe made him look like either a good debtor or a liar, and his lawyer decided to have a conference with him. A false credit statement in writing is bad in Maine. They made over the mortgage, which was really his wife's, to me and I got my claim out of it. He always maintained that I was a crook and he could prove it.

It is a good idea to lock the door before the horse is stolen, but sometimes prompt and effective action will get the horse back. Just what the prompt and effective action is going to be is usually the poser. I was approached one day by a young man who wanted a pair of pants for himself and a pair of shoes for his lady friend. He claimed he was working for a sawmill, and would pay me Saturday when he got his pay. I found out he was a liar, had never worked for the sawmill, had no property, and I was hooked. I did some tall studying on this case and evolved some prompt and effective action that has given good results many times.

In a nearby town was a collection lawyer who had a reputation for sticking to his job. I've heard it said that he had a bill to collect from a man who died, and he attached the casket with the man in it and held up the funeral until the outraged family dug up the amount of the bill. So I wrote a letter to this lawyer, Mr. C. W. Hussey, about as follows:

## CREDIT, GOING AND COMING

Dear Sir:

Henry Pierpoint got these goods from me by lying. This brings him under the statute for getting goods under false pretenses. Now I want you to have him arrested at once, and I will make out a case against him that will keep him in prison for a couple of years. I don't care about the cost. I want to hang him up like a crow in the cornfield to scare the others.

Yours truly,<br>R. E. Gould.

I signed my name to it and put it in an envelope and addressed it as if by error to Henry Pierpoint. The next morning when I opened the store an old woman sat on the steps. She said, "I want to pay a bill that Henry owes, and I want a receipt in full." She got it, and probably is still wondering why the lightning never struck.

I have found it almost impossible to ruin the business by making people pay their bills. Once in a while I stir up a hornet's nest, of course, and wonder whether the gain was worth while. But usually the man who is forced to pay me the bill he owes gets over it. In the long run the results are either that I get rid of a bad customer for good, or he gets over it and forgets. I remember one man who paid me after a suit and came in to abuse me. He said, "I'm square with you and I'm going to stay that way, and I'm going to tell all my friends just what kind of a hairpin you are—and you won't get another cent of my money or theirs."

I said, "Now, Elmer—that is your privilege, and you should do it if you feel like it. But remember that some of the people

# CREDIT, GOING AND COMING

in this town don't like you—and they might be glad to hear what I made you do. Fact is, they might trade with me on that account, and offset your friends."

It took the sweetness out of his abuse for him, and he went out. As far as I know, he never broadcast, because he knew I was right. In two weeks he came into the store purring like a cat over warm milk and bought a big cash order.

## 12

## GOING AFTER IT

TIMES have changed. When I started in business every farm had a good farmer on it. If one of them came in and bought five barrels of flour, a barrel of sugar, a tub of lard, and couldn't pay for it, there wasn't really much to worry about. Next week he'd come in with something from his farm. Every week he had something to sell because he was a farmer and raised things for that purpose. He brought apples, potatoes, eggs, butter, veal, lamb, wood, maple syrup, hay. . . .

In my territory the typical farmer today has a dozen children, a radio with the battery down, an old automobile that won't run, and nothing worth buying. We still see some good ones, of course, but they have become exceptions. For that reason the farmer offers the country storekeeper very few business opportunities. Their credit is generally poor, they have no effects to fall back on, and they have less and less produce to do business with. Instead, most of them work out, and their prosperity goes up and down with the business of the mills where they have jobs. When the mill is running at

## GOING AFTER IT

capacity, they are as good as wheat. When the mill is down, the storekeeper has to harden his heart.

I have always been somewhat of an easy mark for a hard-luck story, and many times I've been skewered like a corned brisket. But I make up for it with the satisfaction that comes with charity—and sometimes I make up for it most pleasantly when my bread returns to me with butter all spread. I remember one young man who came in and asked for credit. I said, "I'm sorry, my boy, but I can't trust you—when you worked you just barely made a living, and now you're out of a job and couldn't possibly pay—I just can't do it."

He said, "You look here, Gould. I've *got* to have this stuff. I've got six children and my wife, and all there is to eat in the house is two soda crackers. My wife has an old pair of felt slippers on her feet, and the children are all barefoot, and all I've got to wear on my feet is these. . . ." He showed me an old pair of lumberman's rubbers that were mostly holes.

When he put it that way there really wasn't much to do. A man as badly off as that can go to the town for aid, and many a storekeeper has buttoned up his heart and sent him. But the truth is that the storekeeper has something of a moral obligation to his community, and sometimes the storekeeper meets his obligations without hope of profit. I told him he could have some stuff that came to $27.65, and he wept all over the store. "I'll pay this," he kept saying, but I couldn't see a chance of ever getting a nickel back. I didn't itemize the goods—merely set down the amount and resolved to remind St. Peter someday if the old chap had missed it.

Two months later a sawmill man came in and said, "How much does Percy owe you?" I looked it up and told him. He said, "How in hell can you make money trusting people like that?"

I became philosophic and went on like this: "I can't, and I can't make money on people like you. You can buy some things as cheap as I can. But between you two is a class I can sell to and make money on. I guess that's all."

He said, "I've got to pay Percy's bill. I want the cuss to do some work for me, and he won't until I pay your bill for him." Percy has always had good credit at my place, and he thinks I'm only a little lower than the angels.

## 13

## FIRST AND SECOND GUESSES

Sometimes a country storekeeper barks up his shins trying to judge the potential paying powers of his customers. One fall an old fellow came in, and I began sizing him up for credit. I had no idea who he was, but I expected him to try and get some goods on time. He priced about everything in the store, and finally asked me the price on whole corn. He was amazed at my price, and said a competitor had offered him corn very much cheaper.

I told him that at that time of year we often got that situation: my corn was number 2, a year old and very dry, but the other merchant had got in a car of new corn. The reason new corn is cheaper is that it will contain 10 to 12 percent more moisture. I never bought new corn early, because if we got a warm spell it would heat. The old fellow shook his head as if he couldn't bring himself to believe such a story, and I decided if he bought anything I'd put the price as low as possible so he might pay cash—and then refuse him credit on such a tight margin.

When he asked me my best price on a hundred bags of

## FIRST AND SECOND GUESSES

corn I did just that. I figured close and hardly left myself a profit. He grunted at the price, and then grinned and said:

"I'll take a hundred bags, and water my horses at the brook." The old cuss had been putting on an act for me! He pulled out a roll of bills as big as a loaf of bread and counted them out on the counter.

Up in Maine we have a lot of French-Canadians, and while I wouldn't want to lay down a rule by which to judge them, my experience has been that among them they know all the ways to skin anybody out of his front teeth. Once I was cheated horribly by a man with a harelip, and I have never been able to trust anyone similarly afflicted to this day, and I may be the same way about French-Canadians. Those who traded with me forty years and always paid have nevertheless been subjected to my doubts. However, as the refrain of a ribald Maine song goes, "You could tell he was a Frenchman by the children on his steps." Big families eat lots of groceries, and I liked to sell them, so I catered to this trade and got my profit as I could. To give them their due, they paid up with me as well as any class—although I probably worked harder for my money in some cases.

One of the most enjoyable challenges I ever had was with one of these people. A young Frenchman moved in, already equipped with enough children to start a school, and he wanted a week's credit. He was working in the paper mill, drove a Ford car, and I said yes. When he didn't pay at the end of the week, I attached the car pronto. I went up with the sheriff to get it, and the fellow came roaring out of his house with, "You can't have him, she's my wife's."

It was registered in his name, so I said we'd take it and he

## FIRST AND SECOND GUESSES

could prove ownership in court. He asked for time and had a talk with his wife, after which he came out and said, "My wife says he'll pay you next Friday, so go home. I don't want all the neighbor to know my whole dam' business."

I told him if he and his wife would give me a mortgage on the car I'd wait. They did, but next rent day he moved, car and all. When I located him in a remote part of town, the car bore a for-sale sign, and he seemed disturbed that I had interfered again. He said he'd pay me when he sold the car. Still anxious to keep a large family on speaking terms, I said I'd wait. It went along for weeks and months, and I found he had given another mortgage on the same car to another grocer —mine was first and was on record. I burned up a lot of gasoline driving back and forth to press my claim, but at last I went down resolved to take the car.

He put up another yell, and finally said, "You give me $60 and you can have him." I said, "No, you give me $25 and you can keep him."

We argued sometime on this, but in the end I took the car. As I was starting it up, he waxed vituperative. He said, "You goddam old son-a-beach, you, you get off my land or I kick you right square in the gut. You make more dam' trouble dan I ever see. You come up to my house so much to take dis car you scare my wife, and when she have baby right on his behind is picture of R. E. Gould." I let out the clutch, and as I cleared the driveway I heard him yell, "I'm goin' sue you for thousand dollar damage."

I never heard anymore about the portrait gallery or the suit for a thousand, but I sold the car and got my money. I put this ad in the local paper:

# FIRST AND SECOND GUESSES

### Unequaled Bargain

I have a Ford car for sale. It is equipped with all modern improvements including first and second mortgages. Mine is the first. This car has already put one family on their feet and it looks as if they would walk for some time. Don't buy a wild young car that may run away and kill you or your family. This one is guaranteed old and steady. The price is $185 but for a quick sale I have decided to take $25, no questions asked or answered. Every week I keep it the price goes down $5, and at the end of three weeks I am going to throw it in the river. Speak quick or you lose him.

A man woke me up at five o'clock the next morning, and I had my $25 in about a minute.

Most methods of recovering a bad debt worked many times afterwards, but there had to be a first and I always felt good when I thought up a new one. One day a driver brought in a big order with the news, "I've got a new customer."

The customer ran a big boarding house, and would pay every Friday, which was payday at the mill where her boarders worked. Friday was payday at the mill, all right, but she didn't come near us. When she hit $40 I called a halt and cast about for a way to bring her in. I got the sheriff to get the names of her boarders, and on the next payday he served trustee writs on them. The woman went up in the air like a balloon and said she would have paid me anyway. I said that was fine, and she dug up the money and paid me to release her boarders—but it was a poor week for her other creditors.

## FIRST AND SECOND GUESSES

My lawyer told me he'd never heard of its being done before. But it has happened since that I know about.

The most far-fetched recourse I ever took was when the station was broken into. A railroad detective came around and looked for clues, but didn't find any. I did. I was walking up the track the day after the break and saw a trail of flour, as if someone had carried a broken bag. Flour had been stolen. I didn't say anything to the detective, since he didn't ask, but I remembered that. When one of my customers who lived along the track took to drinking and went behind in his bill, I cornered him and said, "Fred, you either pay up at once or give me a mortgage on your cow, or I'll write the railroad and tell them about the trail of flour leading into your house."

He swore at me, but came in and signed the mortgage, and eventually he paid it off. The truth is, I saw a trail of flour on the tracks—and never knew whose house it led to. It was a shot in the dark, and it hit the bull's-eye. Actually, a shot in the dark is about the only way to second guess about credit. A lot of my efforts to get the horse back in the barn never worked. I haven't talked much about them.

## 14

## I PAY TO ADVERTISE

I PROBABLY know less than anyone in the world about advertising. Up where I am, a merchant can't hire a smart publicist and let it go at that. But I was in a place where advertising seemed essential, and I took a whirl at it.

I had always felt that a lot of money was wasted on uninteresting copy, and I figured most people like something with a funny slant to it. I kept that in mind as I turned out my weekly copy for Madison *Bulletin*, and although I don't presume to condone my own humor and wit, I will say that my advertising sold goods. I will say that people read the messages. I know that my rhymes were quoted all over town, and occasionally I would learn of their being used in other connections by others with stuff to sell. I have always believed that long before its time I stumbled on an important advertising truth—that a laugh is good for business.

One of my first efforts had to do with butter. I had a refrigerator full of strong butter, and I also had my regular first-grade butter. In August, when feed shortens up, the cows

## I PAY TO ADVERTISE

give less milk, and the effect is a rise in the price of butter. That year it went to sixty cents, and I had a few complaints about the rise. I had a good comeback—I'd give them a pound of my strongest variety for fifty cents, and then they'd be glad to pay sixty cents. This gave me what I thought was an idea, so I wrote out this ad and put it in the *Bulletin:*

> Butter—25¢ a pound!
>
> I have some butter that I will sell for 25¢ a pound. If you don't like it, don't bother to bring it back. Just put it outdoors and say, "Go home!" It is strong enough to walk back and knows the way. If you buy a pound of this butter and like it, I will give you another pound as a premium.
>
> We also have some good butter made by the best butter-makers under sanitary conditions, which costs 60¢ a pound and is worth it. You won't need any premium with this butter to make you feel contented.
>
> R. E. Gould.

Well, this ad pulled big. Everyone came in and demanded a pound of twenty-five-cent butter! If I learned anything, it was that a little nonsense here and there brought in sales from everywhere—and that price was more potent than quality in making sales among my community. I began to shape my advertising policy along those lines.

When everyone was talking about the High Cost of Living, I worked out a method of using current terms in my copy, and began with this:

## I PAY TO ADVERTISE

I had a dream the other night when all around was still.
I dreamed I met old H. C. L. a-coming down the hill,
A profiteer was by her side, a tear was in his eye,
He said, "Gould's cutting prices, Ma," and she said,
"Don't you cry.
Oh, my little son,
Do not weep and curse.
I know he acted bad last week,
But next week he'll do worse."

The town followed down through my list of special bargains for that week. I had more trouble thinking up poetry than I did bargains. It got so the readers wouldn't question my sales claims, but would be put out if I had a poor poem. I exhausted the nursery rhymes in short order:

> Rub-a-dub-dub,
> Two boys in a tub,
> Put there 'cause they have no pants on.
> And there they must stay while mother's away
> Buying clothes at Gould's in Anson.

I barely remember what this advertised:

> Sing a song of six pints,
> Pocket full of rye—
> Hops, malt, and yeast cakes,
> Homebrew by-and-by.
> When the keg was opened they all began to sing,
> How we wish old Volstead
> Had to drink the —— thing.

## I PAY TO ADVERTISE

And children actually repeated this one in the streets:

> Mother, may I go out and flivver?
> Yes, my darling daughter,
> But stop at Gould's, across the river,
> Where you can save a quarter.

> What on? . . . Nearly everything.

I fooled around with things like this for a while, on a sort of cub reporter basis, and suited the dialogue to whatever came to the net. It was months before it occurred to me that I could do a bang-up job on goods now, because I had a reading public. I remember telling myself, "You mustn't let your readers down." And along came the flour situation again. It seems curious to be recalling all the flour episodes in my life—but flour was a constant headache in those days, and I spent a good part of my time thinking about it. After the war flour went sky high, and I figured out something that gave me a real chance to adjudicate my advertising.

Before the war we used to look up the price of wheat per bushel, multiply by five, and add twenty-five cents for milling charge. That gave us the price of flour, delivered. This meant that five bushels of wheat would give us a barrel of flour, and enough stock feed to pay for freight and packages. But now, millers were trying to get a dollar for the milling charge, and feed was very high. My flour business, which had always been good, was definitely in bad shape. I couldn't offer anything every storekeeper in town couldn't match.

It seemed to me, however, that with feed as high as second-grade flour, there wouldn't be too much point in making too

## I PAY TO ADVERTISE

poor a flour. I got some second-grade flour, and puttered around the kitchen making biscuits until I was sure that the present second-grade flour was just about as good as the old standard brands. I thought a good price would make it even better. I bought five carloads of second-grade flour, and it turned out to be tiptop. I had a price of $5 a barrel under the other merchants in town, who were sticking to the old first-grade brands—and my advertising reflected the shine in my eyes. I never felt better in my life.

I started selling flour at $6.50 a barrel—five for $30. This was at a time when other storekeepers were paying $10 simply because they didn't figure things out. I paid $5. The first three cars were sold directly from the freight house. I addressed some cards, and when the freight train passed the junction I dropped the cards in the mail. People who had ordered flour got cards saying, "Your flour is here," and they were lined up along the platform when the train came in. People taking five barrels had to get their last three from later shipments, and I suppose I'm the only man who ever had a waiting list for flour. I exuded good spirits, and rubbed it into the A&P store terribly. I was buying cheaper than they could, because they had a warehouse full to clean up. I sold the five cars and never had a complaint.

It was at this time that the suggestion was heard that they take up the bridge. Madison, across the river, had a lot of storekeepers who saw their customers crossing over to Anson to trade, and taking up the bridge seemed to them like a smart way of counteracting my new zeal for advertising. I don't blame them a bit, I did rub it in. But when they sug-

## I PAY TO ADVERTISE

gested the bridge be taken up, I composed the following and used it to head my next ad:

### The Keeping of the Bridge
#### By R. E. Gould
(Where you got the good flour)

#### With help from Macaulay

When R. E. Gould of Anson bought out the Willis store
He swore that all consumers should suffer wrong no more.
By the nine gods he swore it and marked his prices down,
And every merchant cursed the day when he moved into town.
East and West and North and South
The *Bulletins* go fast,
Till every town and hamlet has heard his trumpet blast.
He cut dry goods wide open,
He made the clothiers yell,
And he printed foolish poetry that made folks laugh like fun.

Just then a scout came flying all wild with haste and fear,
"Gould's bought a stock of boots and shoes,
And they will soon be here!"
On the low hills to westward the merchant fixed his eye
And saw a swarthy storm of dust rise fast along the sky.
And nearer yet and nearer doth that dread whirlwind come;
And louder yet and still more loud
From underneath that rolling cloud
Was heard a voice like trumpet loud,
Inviting folks to come.

## I PAY TO ADVERTISE

"Rubber boots made on the square,
The kind that come clear up to there
For only three-and-a-half a pair.
Why don't you all buy some?"

It was really a long time before I was 100 percent welcome among the tradesfolk of Madison after that, but we have frequently chummed around since and they all laugh about taking up the bridge.

At about this time the weather conspired to teach me that I had the kind of advertising I needed, and that I could forget about the ordinary kind. I bought the materials for a ready-made sale. A New York house sold me all the goods and a thousand circulars all printed with pictures and prices. They threw in decorative banners. It was to be a *Rainbow Sale*. My store was decorated like the coat of many colors, and the sale started off without too much promise. I was discouraged. Then the last of the week the heavens opened and my rainbow sale was completely rained out. A few watersoaked customers came in to get essential groceries, but my special stock of goods was still on the shelves.

So I reserved a place in the *Bulletin,* and announced that my rainbow sale would, because of the weather, be continued another week—and that the name was now changed to *Rain Sale*. I dwelt on the fact that the enlarged Kennebec River had backed up the drains, and stated that "Anyone buying over five dollars' worth of goods will be given a free boat ride in my cellar." The waterlogged community, most of whose homes were at least partly flooded, was glad to see a chance to smile, and bright and early Monday morning my store was

## I PAY TO ADVERTISE

jammed and the rainbow sale broke all records. I never again wrote an ad that failed to contain what I call humor—and I have never since written an ad that didn't do more than I hoped it would.

People have called attention to the fact that Raymond's, in Boston, copies my style when they advertise with "Uncle Eph." I found myself writing ads that were only remotely concerned with selling goods—and they sold goods just the same.

One spring I bought space and centered this:

### Ode to the Ford Car

Lizzie, Lizzie, Fuel Eater—
She was a Ford, you couldn't beat her.
Up the hill she wouldn't go so well,
But downhill she would go like sixty.

I hope your Ford wintered well,
And you will drive around and see me soon.

I observed, when the paper came out, that I had neglected to add my signature—but people came in chuckling and acted as if they hadn't noticed it. My efforts were not literary, but they served my purpose. This one was from a long poem on radios:

One night they had a wedding,
You could hear 'em just as plain.
We heard the fellow say "I do,"
And the organ pealed again.
And then a girl said,

## I PAY TO ADVERTISE

"George and I put rice in her umbrella,"
And mother sighed and said, "Poor girl,"
And Pa said, "Huh! Poor fella!"

Why such foolishness should increase my sales of dry goods is something I don't know. I merely know it did, and I know it got people into the habit of reading my ads. I got to the point where I'd invest in a huge space and then crowd something like this into the corner in small type:

### Ladies' Hats

Your choice .............................. $3.00
My choice .............................. $1.50

A lady misunderstood this and wanted to pick out one for $1.50. She said she'd rather pay ten dollars for a hat than take one I picked out as a present. But then, I am not much of a hat merchant.

R. E. Gould,
Anson, Maine.

I bought some men's pants once, just because I had visualized the following:

### Easy to Sell

During the hard times of 1908 I was traveling in New York State. Every drummer had a hard luck story to tell. We met one old fellow who said business was good with him. He said, "They arrest people if they don't buy my goods." We asked him what he sold, and he said,

## I PAY TO ADVERTISE

### "MEN'S PANTS!"

Don't wait until you are arrested.

| | |
|---|---|
| Work pants | $1.50 |
| Montana kersey | 2.00 |
| All wool khaki | 2.50 |
| Young men's pants in fancy stripes and serges | 4.00 |

Lots of better ones, and some cheaper.

I began to work my stuff around so that I took customers into my confidence—a mighty fine system. In the battles that waged among merchants, the readers felt they were on my side. A battle over tea was going on, and I went to press with this:

There was an old man from Tarentum,
He gnashed his false teeth till he bent 'em,
When folks bought a pound of Gould's tea, he found
They liked it. He couldn't prevent 'em.

### TEA

If you had been selling tea for 80¢ a pound, and another fellow offered a pound of tea and a 75¢ dishpan for 50¢, you would be mad, too. Did you know I have the largest rug department in New England? All outdoors. Come and see the rugs hung up out of doors. The sun won't hurt good carpets.

When wool goods shot up, I had a stock on hand, and I advertised like this:

What do you know about wool? It grows on sheep and is worth 20¢ a pound. Then how much is an all wool

## I PAY TO ADVERTISE

sweater worth that weighs three pounds? $9. Whoa! Back up! Your arithmetic is wrong but your price is correct. But it doesn't sound right to me. I have some wool goods I bought last January, and I am going to sell them just as if I could buy more.

I followed that with straight prices, and the next week I tried the same tactics on shoes—which were selling for ten dollars when calfskins were worth about one and one-half cents a pound:

> What do you know about shoes? Come away, children. I don't know if this man has corns or has just discovered that it takes 83 calf skins to buy a pair of shoes.

And so my advertising campaign unfolded. I found I could sell almost anything by getting a slant on it—and when I was desperate one week I even did the following:

> The Junebug's wings are lined with gold,
> The Lightning bug's with flame.
> The bed bug's got no wings at all—
> But he gets there just the same.

That's the way with my advertising. It doesn't look very well or sound very good, but it produces results.

Of all the ads I ever ran, I have a liking for one I did on flour. It combined a chatty tone with the old confidence routine, and it moved a healthy lot of flour. Each of my competitors has commented on it since, and dozens of customers have admitted it was the first time they ever understood the flour situation. Here it is:

# I PAY TO ADVERTISE

### Flour Facts and Feed

Oh, say can you see
   By the dawn's early light
Gould rolling out flour
   And Carl at the teaming,
People hollering for more
   Who've already had four,
And a girl at the door
   With a biscuit all steaming?

Wheat has been selling for $1 a bushel for a long time. Wheat feeds are very high. $1 wheat used to mean $5 flour. I am selling a barrel of good flour for $6.50, and lots of folks are saying it can't be done. I will give you the inside facts and let you be the judge.

270 pounds of wheat is 4½ bushels

| | | |
|---|---:|---:|
| 4½ bushels of wheat is | | $4.50 |
| 270 pounds of wheat makes | | |
|   Flour, pounds | 196 | |
|   Feed, pounds | 72 | |
|   Shrinkage, pounds | 2 | |
| | 270 | |
|   Milling cost | | .50 |
|   Packages | | .30 |
|   Freight to Anson | | .90 |
| | | $6.20 |
| Less 72 pounds of feed at $1.80 cwt. | | 1.29 |
| | | $4.91 |

## I PAY TO ADVERTISE

The miller wants a profit, and so does the traveling man. Some millers make a short patent flour and get a big price for it. Just what do they do? They take 20 pounds of low grade flour out of each barrel. Do they throw it away?

### THEY DO NOT

They put it into a Baker's Clear and get almost as much for it as for any flour. Suppose they put it into middlings? It wouldn't make over 20¢ difference on a barrel. We will allow 9¢ for the miller and 5¢ for the salesman, and 20¢ for the fancy patent, and we have $5.25 as the cost of a good barrel of flour. I will leave it to you if I can't sell it for $6.50. I have just put out one car, and am taking orders for the next car to arrive in Oct. 1. I believe flour is on the bargain counter. I have increased my order to 1,000 barrels. I look for a drop in the price of feed right away. If it drops, flour will be higher. I think you will do well to come in and place your order for what you will need for a year. Come in and see some biscuits I made from this flour. If you are not suited, money refunded and no charge for what you have used.

Well, they came, and they bought flour. And the other storekeepers, who had paid too much for flour, would gladly have cut my throat. As I read the ad over now, I wonder why they didn't.

## 15

## THE BOARD OF EDUCATION

THE storekeeper naturally gets to enjoy prominence in his town. Around his stove, of an evening, he hears the gossip of the community, and just before town meeting he listens to heated arguments about politics. It is wise to listen, but not take part. I would rather sell groceries to John Brown than correct his warped views of the party in power. To correct his views might lead him to trade across the street, at least until after town meeting. But several times in my life I have been induced to run for office. I doubt now if it ever seriously affected my merchandising, but it might have, and I probably was unwise to participate.

As a selectman, I was called upon to settle many local matters that required real tact for one in business. I occasionally threw tact out of the window and jumped on someone's toes —and when I did it to the wrong person I decided not to run again. I did, once, run for the school board in Anson—and have always been glad. To be sure, I came out of it with bitterness toward our professional educators, and I learned what is chiefly wrong with our schools. It was not a happy

## THE BOARD OF EDUCATION

time, but I often wished I were better qualified to conduct a crusade to improve conditions. Teachers, as a class, are constitutionally disqualified from teaching through the scarcity of their real life experiences; and the stringent rules of the state-wide system binds them down even further. I know this because I saw it. I have no right to complain, perhaps, because I don't know what to do about it. My few positive suggestions would do some good if the educated teachers would listen to me, but I could never hope to rearrange the theory of schooling. I will say that for my part I think the teaching in the elementary subjects is hopelessly improper, and I have proved to myself that the country storekeeper can sometimes do a better teaching job than the schools.

The first day I kept store in Anson a half-pint stuttering French boy followed me around all day making funny noises. At last he got it out, "D-d-d-do you w-w-w-want to huh-huh-huh-hire a man?" I said, "Who?" He said, "Mm-m-me!" I had a job about his size and I tried him out. When he finished it, he found something else to do. At the end of the week he was on the force. I gave him fifty cents a day, and he worked before and after school hours, and all day Saturdays. He was delighted, and his loyalty was wonderful. I found, early, however, that his manners needed a little correction.

Our immediate neighborhood was composed almost entirely of French-Canadians and Slavs or frogs and squareheads, as they called each other. Every time a Slavic child came in the store Chippie would say, "Ish do peckler!" I noticed the effect, and I asked, "Chip, what does that mean?" He said, "Oh, that's squarehead, and it means 'go to hell!'"

I said, "Now, Chip, we don't want to say things like that to

## THE BOARD OF EDUCATION

our customers; we want them to come back and spend their money here." So the next time a squarehead youngster came in, I almost threw a fit when I heard Chip say, "Ish do North Anson!" He turned to me and explained inter-community feeling by saying, "That's much worse." However, I got Chippie so he understood the cooperative spirit that small towns, and larger ones too, must promote. I thought to myself, "Why don't the public schools bring these two people together better?" And I have never been answered.

Chip took to storekeeping. He stayed in the store until the last bell, and ran all the way to school. He came home from school at four in the afternoon, and stayed until we closed. One afternoon he turned up missing. He ran in out of breath at five, and I said, "Where've you been?"

"I h-h-h-had to stay after skoo-skoo-school!"

"What was the matter?"

"Th-th-that god-dam' l-l-l-long division."

After supper I had Chip come back, and he and I leaned over the counter and investigated the woes of long division. I found out he couldn't subtract. I formed my opinion of a teacher who tried to teach long division to a boy who couldn't subtract. I finally got Chip so he could take 39 from 86, and he sailed along in arithmetic until he came to fractions.

Again we leaned over the counter, and stayed there until midnight trying to make sense out of fractions. It just didn't register. The boy wasn't equal to it. I said, "Chip, go on home—I don't believe you'll ever know what a fraction is." I thought, maybe it isn't the teacher's fault after all—some things are just impossible.

The next morning Chip was present, and so was a man

## THE BOARD OF EDUCATION

with a hog. I asked Chip to weigh the hog, and he came in with a slip of paper and reported, "Huh-huh-he weighs 197½ pounds."

I said, "How much does that come to at ten cents a pound?"

Quicker than scat Chip said, "$19.75."

I said, "Now, Chip, how does it happen that you know what half a pound of hog is at ten cents a pound, but you don't know what a fraction is?" Chip said, "Is that all there is to it?"

And from then on he did fractions with the best of them. I rearranged my opinion of teachers again—it wasn't impossible; it was simply a matter of method. I'd tried too hard; so had the teacher. Neither of us had thought of weighing a hog, literally or figuratively. Chip could do fractions all the time—but no one had ever defined them to his liking.

One day Chip didn't go to school, and about eleven o'clock I found him waiting on trade. "Did you forget to go to school?"

Chip said, "No, my fa-fa-father says I learn more here than I dud-dud-do in school." So I went to see his teacher, and she seemed to think as much, in a weary sort of way that I have come to associate with teachers. She sent me to the superintendent. He said to let Chip stay in the store until I heard from him. Chip should live so long. Twenty years have passed, and no word yet. Chip stayed in the store, and I made sure that he kept on with reading, writing, spelling, and arithmetic. He left me in a few years, and now has a responsible position with a large corporation. Chip had little schooling, but he got a good education.

## THE BOARD OF EDUCATION

That, really, was the way it all started. The next March a member of the school board refused to run again, and I was nominated. There was no opposition, and it looked like a good chance to find out about some things that had always made me wonder. Remembering Chippie I went down to the fifth grade soon after I was sworn in and asked to see some of the written work in mathematics. Out of 34 papers I found 12 that indicated that the pupils had never learned to subtract. I jotted down the names and went to visit some parents. The teacher was honest enough; she said, "I know, they should have got subtraction last year, but they didn't—and I haven't time to do it this year in addition to my regular work."

To the parents I carried the information that their children were failing because they couldn't subtract. "Now I'm just a storekeeper, but all my life I've had to do number work. I can teach your youngster what he doesn't know quicker than the schools can." Then I'd suggest that they send their youngsters to the store at 6:00 P.M., and I'd spend an hour or two each evening with them.

Eight youngsters came the first night, but before I got through I had 25—and today I'll stack their arithmetic up against the best the schools ever turned out. I soon weeded out those who needed help from those who didn't try, and after a few nights I introduced the Board of Education. I got a half-inch board about four feet long and about four inches wide. I whittled a handle on it. Then when the class assembled I very ostentatiously drove a nail into the floor.

Then I said, "Now I am done fooling and telling you what to do. The next person who neglects to borrow ten to make

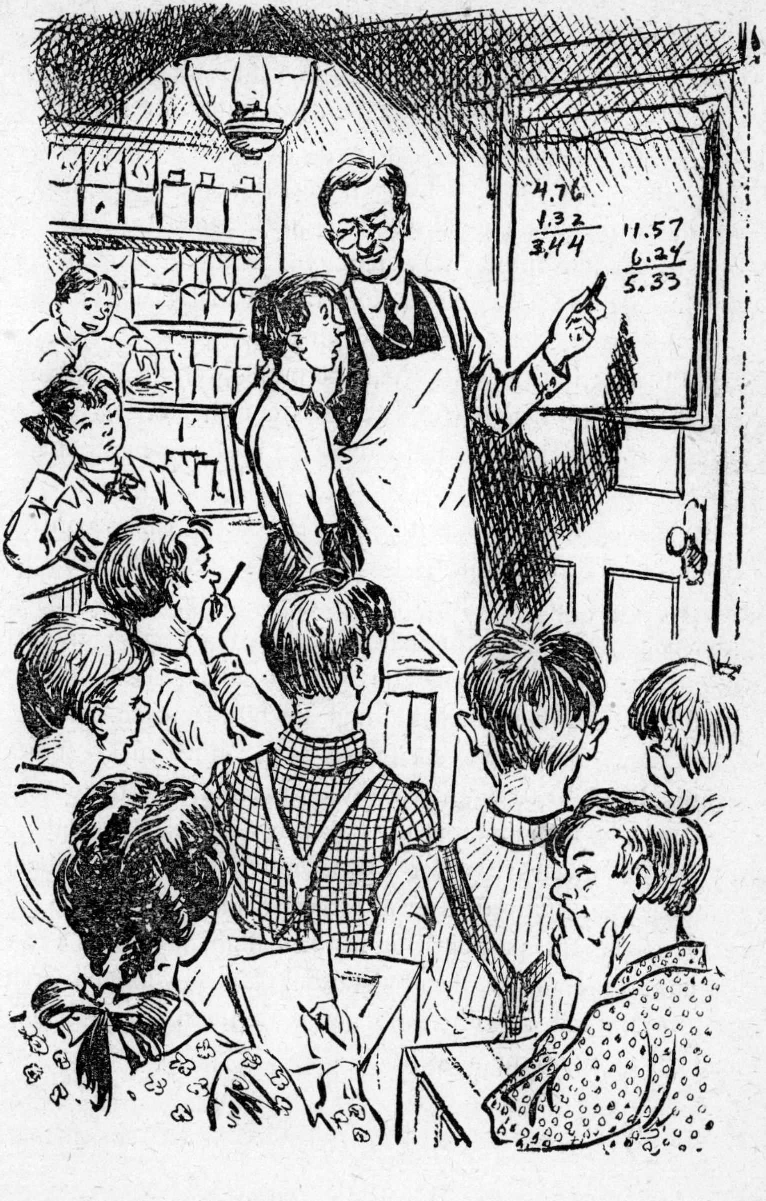
4.76
1.32
3.44
11.57
6.24
5.33

## THE BOARD OF EDUCATION

it possible to take nine from six or to pay it back when he subtracts the second figure will go over and put his finger on that nail. The executioner will then give him a good one with the Board of Education."

I named one boy executioner, and pretty soon he had a customer. Then the one who had just been executed took over the paddle and lay in wait for the next one. Once a boy got his previous executioner. Oh, boy! What a whack! But after a few more lessons my class broke up. It wasn't much of a job to teach arithmetic when the pupils were really trying. I don't know whether the teachers know that or not, but I can attest that the Board of Education is a sovereign remedy for failing memory.

I had a son then, about ten, and I used the same board to make him recall his duties toward the woodbox. I spoke to him several times, but he still "forgot," and one night I made him put his finger on the nail. He never forgot again. Indeed months afterward he spoke to me about putting the hairbrush up on the bathroom shelf too high for him to reach. I would put it down on a lower shelf for a time, and then I'd forget again. He spoke to me several times, but I still "forgot," and one night he made me put my finger on the nail. I tingled for two days, and have never forgotten the great educational stimulation I received. I never forgot again.

Of course, this participation in town affairs had some effect on business. I was thanked by grateful parents whose children were promoted on time, and a few of them stopped long enough to buy some groceries.

## 16

## I CATCH A THIEF

I DON'T know what other stores do about shoplifters, and lacking this information I had to find my own method. Every store is bothered with them, and I've always thought swiping things from a store counter is a special kind of larceny. There must be a sporting element to it that attracts. I may be biased, but I seem to recall that the worst offenders in my experience all looked pious and incapable of naughty actions. Also, it is hard to bring yourself to be suspicious and watch the town's leading citizens— but the leadingest citizen is capable of it now and then according to my records.

We'd miss an item here and an item there, and we'd watch —but we couldn't seem to connect with the guilty party. Many times there seemed to be no reason for it—after we'd had nothing but tobacco and grocery customers, we'd lose a woman's hat. With no one in the store but dry goods customers, we'd miss a box of prunes. As I say, I think many times the thief just takes something for the sake of taking

## I CATCH A THIEF

something—and it's difficult to detect and rationalize that sort of thievery.

After a few items had been reported stolen, I opened a running account with Thief & Co. Then we went along a year or so charging up hammers, axes, saws, screwdrivers, pants, hose, handkerchiefs, canned goods, tubs of lard, and pounds of this and that. It got to be quite an account, and one day we caught a fellow red-handed. I confronted him with the total of the Thief & Co. account, and he squirmed like a palsied eel. But I never knew one to refuse to pay. If it looked at all stormy I'd say, "I think the best way will be to get a search warrant and search your house." The culprit, who didn't want his neighbors to see the sheriff coming to visit, would scream, but he'd pay.

One day the bookkeeper beckoned me and said, "That man stuck a pound of butter under his coat." We had a nice brand of creamery butter, but this man ran a hotel, and he claimed our price was too high. I had some cheaper butter for his hotel, but it appeared he liked to taste some good stuff occasionally, because I followed him out and sure enough—there was no doubt but that the bundle under his coat was butter. I told the bookkeeper to send him a bill for 100 pounds of butter. He paid without a murmur.

I've made it a practice to say to guilty persons, when they paid up, "Now, as long as you trade here I won't mention this," and I've had numerous lifetime customers.

When I went into the Harmony store I found a box of peanuts in the shell behind the counter. Rats had taken them all around the place, and I couldn't look behind anything but I found a barrel or so of peanut shells. I put the peanuts in

## I CATCH A THIEF

front of the counter. The old proprietor warned me it wouldn't work because the boys would steal them. It seemed to me it made little difference whether the rats or the boys stole them, if that was the case, but I told him I didn't want to run a store that would be sunk by a boy stealing peanuts. As I figured, the peanuts began to sell. Nearly everyone who came in would take a peanut, and as is the nature of the fruit, nearly everyone who took a peanut would buy a bag. They carried a large profit, and I was glad to donate one peanut for the sake of selling a bag full.

However, some people began to abuse their privileges. One big gawk of a high school boy would come in every noon and fill his pockets. My wife noticed this and said, "Why don't you do something to stop it?" She insisted the few abuses were taking the profit. So the next morning I fixed up my basket of peanuts as usual, with a few teasers in the middle, and five-cent bags all around the edge. Anyone could lift off a peanut or two all right, but if anyone gouged in for a handful—I had a steel trap planted down under to protect my interests.

The store filled with customers, and I had my mind taken off the peanut situation until the middle of the forenoon. I was bagging some potatoes when I heard a snap and a scream, and I knew I had caught my thief. It was my wife. I never did fix that one up—when I tried to tell her I was sorry I'd remember how she looked, and laugh all over again. But she served my purpose, because it went all over town that Ralph Gould had caught his wife stealing peanuts, and after that nobody took more than one or two. I've made some dollars selling peanuts to people who stole the first one.

## I CATCH A THIEF

An old lady who used to come to town to sell butter and eggs was a pest and a sort of a thief. She'd hit my store about noon and make some small purchase such as a pound of tea. Then she would grab a couple of pilot biscuits and run for the cheese case. She'd grab a knife and jab it into the cheese and cut out at least a half pound, and this made her lunch. When she got through we'd have to trim away another half pound to satisfy the next customer—who couldn't be blamed for disliking twice the amount of rind he should have had.

I studied the case of the cheese-swiping old woman for a long time, and then one day my heart lit up and radiated joy all over. We had a very firm cheese of light yellow color. We also had some Goodwill soap about the same color. The next time I saw the old lady on her way to my place, I took a bar of Goodwill soap and cut out a wedge of it. I also cut a wedge out of the cheese, and inserted the soap wedge daintily. I cleaned up all the scraps and hid the knife. In she came, and she fell for it. She gagged and sputtered and coughed and hid behind a pile of canned goods until the spasm passed. She finally came out, paid for her pound of tea, and I never saw her in my store again.

Pilferers sometimes present a more difficult problem. I used to have a peephole in the wall of my office, and numerous times I'd spy on an off chance. One night I saw some very good customers come into the store—two sisters who bought big orders and settled every payday. With them, on their shopping visits, was their elderly mother—who always wore a long cloak drawn about her. As I peeped out it came to me suddenly that I was getting the old routine—the sisters paid their bill and gave next week's order while the old woman wandered about the store. As I watched she rolled up a pair

## I CATCH A THIEF

of stockings and slipped them under her cloak. Then she wandered out to the front door and waited around for the girls.

I was stumped. They were good customers, and I hated to lose them. I felt sure they knew of the old lady's activities. I couldn't stand the loss, however, and something had to be done. I finally told the clerks to estimate what the old lady took, to keep an eye on her always, and to make a mistake in adding up the weekly bill—enough to cover what she got. We went along this way for years—they were convinced they were putting one over on me, and they never complained of a mistake in arithmetic. I guess that was as good a way to handle it as I could have found.

One day little Chippie came running into my office and cried, "Juh-juh-juh-jim has stole a sus-sus-sus-sweater!" He pointed out the office window—and sure enough there was Big Jim hurrying up the track with a bulge under his coat. The belt of a lady's sweater of a very vivid salmon pink was hanging out and flopping behind him like a tail.

These sweaters hadn't been selling well—they were too high priced, and were colored a trifle too gay for some of my trade. I was glad I'd found a customer. I went out to the old man's account and charged up, "Sweater, $9." In a few days his wife came in—she was the financier of the family—and she said, "Mr. Gould, awful mistake in my bill." I got out the account and went over the items and finally came to the sweater. "I never had him," she said. "Jim got it," I told her. "He didn't say anything about it, but I saw him going with it, and I charged it." She said, "I find out about dis, ba gosh!" and away she went. Inside a half hour she was back. "Ba gosh, you right, Mr. Gould. Jim did steal it, and he give

## I CATCH A THIEF

it to Mrs. Benson!" Her voice rose to a shriek. She clenched her fists, "I lick him good for dat!" I guess she did, because I heard he cultivated Mrs. Benson less enthusiastically after that, and I know it was two years before he came in my store again.

Through the years we had plenty of instances of men stealing tobacco, and we made them pay. Insecticides and stuff in the back store were always missing. Friday nights, if oysters were left over, we'd pack them in ice and set them on the far back steps of the store overnight. Occasionally I thought someone was cagily taking a few, but when a whole gallon disappeared I had to find another storage place. I told the clerks I'd find out who stole the oysters—some day.

And one day I did. I was checking invoices on some fishing tackle, and got called to the phone. When I came back a box of flies was missing. I recalled who had been around, made a guess on a boy, and rushed up to his house. I asked his mother if he'd brought home a box of flies, and she brought them out to me. I told her she'd better have the boy come and see me, and I sat and talked with him for an hour. He confessed to taking many things I hadn't missed, including the oysters. I jotted down a few prices, and figured he had taken about $20 worth.

"Now," I said, "I'm going to sentence you to hard labor. You go get a job, and start paying back this money. I want at least $2 a week, and I'm not fooling."

Within a week I got a money order for $20, and I receipted the bill. It surprised me, and it was a year or so later that I learned the whole story. The boy broke into a house and stole the money to pay me.

## 17

## COST MARKS AND SELLING PRICES

No matter what a thing sells for, the most important figure connected with it is the original cost. Keeping that figure from the customer would be easy if the storekeeper could leave his figures and invoices locked in the safe. But in a business like mine—where the selling price is usually knocked down and dragged around for dickering purposes—the cost price must be constantly in mind. This calls for a cost mark—a secret among the owner and clerks by which they can compute on the job. The cost mark is an unknown quantity to chain store managers, whose prices are set and immutable, but in my store we had a cost mark in code and except on staple items we seldom put down any actual selling price with a definite and unquestionable finality. We are a trading people up here.

When a customer looked at a box of shoes, he saw something like this:

$$\frac{\text{ALH}}{\$5.69}$$

# COST MARKS AND SELLING PRICES

To the customer, this meant that he could offer five dollars even and sometimes get a trade. To me, it meant the shoes cost $2.25, and I could let them go for anything above that amount and break even. This sort of selling is predicated on the belief that no one will pay the quoted price, but if someone agreed to the full $5.69 I seldom complained. But to be ready for all the vagaries of trading in my area, I kept the actual costs coded on goods and acted accordingly.

My particular cost mark was somewhat different from most. Most are a word of ten letters, no two alike, each letter representing a number:

REPUBLICAN         PERTH AMBOY
1234567890         1234 5 6 7890

Some have nine letters, an X standing for zero:

SKOWHEGAN
123 4 5 6 78 9X

Another is the old tick-tack-toe form:

$$\begin{array}{c|c|c} 1 & 2 & 3 \\ \hline 4 & 5 & 6 \\ \hline 7 & 8 & 9 \end{array}$$

Representing each number by the arrangement of lines around it, the cost marks look like something from the Hindu. Thus, $2.25 becomes ⊔ ⊔ ▫. But the goods in my store were always marked with my own symbols, and possibly some of my old customers—now that they know it—will comment on its appropriateness:

# COST MARKS AND SELLING PRICES

## BACKHOUSE
## 1 2 3 4 5 6 7 8 9

We used X for zero, and L for a repeater—$2.25 would be AAH, but with a repeater it became ALH. As I enlarged my business and first took on a girl clerk I stammered and stuttered all around trying to explain this indelicate business routine to her. Afterward, I realized it bothered me more than it did her. I think women understand such things very well.

This cost business once led a man to say I was a crook because I had two prices. I told him I was crookeder than that as I really had four prices; one for the man who pays cash, one for the man who settles on payday, one for the man who pays when I dun him, and one for the man who doesn't pay until he's sued. Of course, this means that I go around all the time suiting my prices to the kind of fellow I'm dealing with. If I have a mackinaw in stock that cost $2.25, I would sell it for three dollars to a cash customer. But when a tough, long-winded one comes in, I pick it up and look at the cost mark carefully and say, "Six ninety-eight—call it six seventy-five." Usually he says all right and the anticipated profit goes on the books for a long haul.

This kind of sales psychology depends on a little acting, as well as knowing the cost and the customer. A grocer up in Athens used to do a big business with the Tuttles and Browns, and he held it in spite of competition. His method was suited to the people he dealt with. One time pork was selling for ten cents a pound. A competitor had a big sign in the window, "Pork, 9¢ lb." A drummer heard the conversation. A

## COST MARKS AND SELLING PRICES

West Athenite came in and asked, "Bill, what are *you* getting for salt pork?" Bill said, "Seven cents." The man said, "I want a junk." Bill hauled out a piece, put it on the scales, and said, "Just seven pounds—seven times seven is seventy-seven—gimme 75¢." The West Athenite said, "Bill's a good feller to do business with—he always takes off something for cash."

The facts about prices are best kept within the lore of the storekeeper. The buying public isn't too capable of assimilating them. That is why we frequently hear people complain it is dishonest to charge two prices on the same goods. For my part, I simply know too steep a price will keep the cash man from buying, and if I sell the long-winded fellow he isn't looking for price—he's looking for credit, and if you take him on at all you want to allow leeway so the eventual profit is worth waiting for. If a man hasn't a fair shade of the Yankee trader in him he'd better keep away from country store business.

Once I was visiting a store in another town, and as we talked the proprietor reached down in the bone box under the meat counter and brought up some bones. He had the arch bone from the rump with all the meat cut off, and two calf legs cut off at the knee. He laid them on the counter. I looked out the door to see who was coming, and I saw a noted pest tying his horse. He was one of those men who come in, eat a frankfurt and a handful of raw hamburg, price everything, then go out saying you are too high. He came in and asked, "What have you got for meat?"

My storekeeper friend looked around and discovered a bargain. He pointed at the three waste bones. "There's a

## COST MARKS AND SELLING PRICES

good trade, there—you can have the whole business for fifty cents." The old pest said, "I'll give you ten cents." My friend said, "All right, seeing it's you. Take 'em." The man was satisfied, and the storekeeper got ten cents for some bones he planned to throw away. True, the customer got some decent soup bones, but he also was the victim of a trader smarter than he was. Ordinarily we hate to fool around with that kind of trade, but it serves to keep us on our toes, and maybe shows why we need more than one kind of price.

I remember one old man who abused us severely. He called us thieves and robbers and found fault with everything in the store. Finally one of the clerks refused to wait on him. I said, "All right—I'll wait on him. He doesn't bother me a bit. If you'll notice, when he gets through cussing at us, he hauls out a roll of bills and says 'how much' and pays. I like that kind better than the pleasant sort who says 'charge it' and never plans to pay."

That kind of a fellow we can quote a decent price. Once in a while, though, we find a fellow trying to dicker us down on something we haven't allowed margin enough on. I remember one time a man came in and asked, "What you got to keep a feller's feet warm?" I got out his size in the best thing ever devised to protect the feet—the Maine woodsman's standby, felt boots. Then there were all-wool hose, a pair of felt shoes lined with sheepskin with the wool on, then a pair of felt-lined high overshoes. He put them on and admired them. He said, "Them ought to do it, all right." He waited a minute, not able to bear the thought, and then he plunged right in, "How much?"

I looked at my cost marks, figured a cash price as close as

## COST MARKS AND SELLING PRICES

I dared, and said, "Six ninety-five, call it six-fifty." He howled like a wounded lion, called me a robber, and indicated he might be interested at five dollars. At times I enjoy rising to such occasions.

"I tell you what I'll do," I said. "Up in Dud Whitney's store in Cambridge I saw three pairs of cowhide boots. Now I'll buy you a pair of them and give them to you, and you can wear them all winter and it won't cost you a cent." He shuddered all over and said, "I couldn't do it." I said, "Of course you could—I've done it, and I know you have. Just get them big so you can wear two pairs of socks, and grease them with mutton tallow every night, and I wouldn't be surprised if you could get two winters out of them."

He shuddered again and said, "Maybe I could, but I'm damned if I will." He shelled out six-fifty and went home without a word. Cowhide boots! I wore them as a boy. The thought of them in below-zero weather will chill a man to his soul. I can remember how they froze up on my feet and I'd bang them against a stump to restore the circulation. Cost prices don't mean a thing when a man is buying felt boots in Maine.

Of course, on staple groceries where the prices are general knowledge we can't quote double or triple prices. But ours was a general trade, and before the customer got out we had injected enough articles of unknown value to suit whatever kind of deal we were engaged in.

One other thing that makes cost prices, always at hand, an essential item is what might be called the psychology of sales. This is something that raises Ned wherever people get together and organize a cooperative store. They may be ready

## COST MARKS AND SELLING PRICES

to save a little money in theory, but in practice they still operate on the old idea that you get what you pay for. The truth is that people *think* they get what they pay for full as often as they don't, and this makes them happy even if they have been skun out of their eye teeth. People pay a price that, as often as not, is based on how much the traffic will stand, and I learned that when I bought out the undertaker at Harmony and found six sewing machines in the stock.

I figured these were a little out of my line, and I decided to price them for a quick sale. What I didn't know was the sales psychology connected with buying things like sewing machines. These six machines were made by a well-known manufacturer and were the exact duplicate of machines accredited agents sold house-to-house at from $40 to $80. The price range depended on the number of attachments (which are hardly ever used) and the number of drawers in the stand. Any machines the accredited agents can't sell are wholesaled to dealers under another name. They cost from $13.50 to $18.75.

I picked out a customer, a young man just married and priced him a machine of the best type at $25. He didn't take it. Pressed for reasons, he finally said his wife said they couldn't be any good at that price. Her chum had one that cost $80 and she wanted one of those. So I put my price up to $80 and eventually sold them. Sewing machines are seldom sold for cash. They have a long-time sale and have to carry a big profit to make them worthwhile.

## 18

## QUEER CHARACTERS

THE country storekeeper gets to thinking everybody is a little queer, and then along comes one of the town heroes just reeking with the stuff characters are made of. It brightens life a lot. Harmony was founded by one of the greatest characters that ever lived, and it was only natural future generations should try to keep up the reputation. The pioneer who settled the town was a young man looking for a good spot to found a dynasty, and he chose a nice place with water power in the center of what is now the town. When he got a rude cabin built he started back to civilization to get his wife. On the way he met a man who had come to tell him his wife had given birth to a baby, and had died.

Three weeks later the sorrow-ridden husband returned to his chosen spot, driving a yoke of oxen who drew a cart loaded with everything in the world the man owned—including the three-weeks-old baby, who made most of the trip in the father's arms. When character material is sought, you can't beat that much. His only neighbors were Indians and his only salvation was his own belief in a bright and glorious future.

Certainly, the baby lived. He grew up and was an officer in the Civil War. The father married another woman who bore him seven children. Then she died, and he married a third woman who brought up the eight. The men in the early days were crazy enough to tackle back- and heart-breaking tasks—but it must be significant that they never wanted for women to help them. Anyway, the job that wore out three women had no damaging effects on our hero, and he lived to see his town develop and his family make a significant mark in the world. They were musicians, painters, poets—all gifted and all a trifle eccentric. When one of the sons lay dying, his sister said to him, "Wal, Cyrus, you'll soon be on the other shore and you'll see Uncle Hiram, and Uncle Ezra, and Uncle Nathan."

Cyrus opened one eye, looked at her steadily, and said, "Yes, and the devil." He never spoke again. The old progenitor, though, was a determined man, and he hated to have his plans go awry. The store that I later bought was a partner in one of his escapades that is still spoken of in that country.

The old fellow had built an enormous house on the hill, and the chambers were outfitted according to the time. Under each bed was a crockery receptacle that probably needs no further identification. Cleanliness was next to godliness, and the women of the house, after the Monday wash was out, would gather the chamber mugs of the house and boil them out. When boiled they were set in the sun in a retiring position behind the house to dry. That morning the mugs had been boiled.

## QUEER CHARACTERS

The old gentleman, with the determined disposition, walked out behind the house and discovered a crow in the kitchen garden pulling up the corn. The old gentleman reached down and grasped a mug by the handle, swung it handily, and hurled it at the crow. He missed, and the crow flew away. This vexed the old fellow; his aim was faltering; he must practice up. So he gave his hired man five dollars and sent him down to the store to buy five dollars' worth of cheap chamber mugs.

The hired man entered into the spirit of the occasion, and at the store he strung the pots on a rope and festooned them about his person in a ludicrous and uncustomary manner. As he clanked up the hill like a knight in armor, the ladies gasped and the men haw-hawed and the light-minded schoolgirls giggled. When the hired man got to the house the old gentleman threw all the mugs at a rock, perfecting his aim in the event he ever had another crow.

One time the old man stood a ladder against his house to fix a sticking window, and the top of the ladder punched out a light of glass. He grabbed the ladder away at the clinking sound, swung it back against the house and punched out another light. This disturbed him to such an extent he went all the way around the big house, punching second story windows out with the end of the ladder. When he got back to the window that stuck he slammed the ladder against the house viciously and yelped, "Now see if you can stand without breaking glass."

One old man who traded with me was a dandy. He owned a woodlot, and lived in a little camp on the lot. He cut wood all fall and early winter, and then went out and bought a horse. He never would pay over $5, and as horses were easy to get at that time of year he always got a horse. Then he would yard out his wood, and, that done, would kill the horse and bring me the skin. He always asked $5 for the skin, and I always gave him his price. People said he ate the horse all winter, but I don't know about that. He'd buck and split wood all winter, and he always had dry wood to sell to those who had cash.

There were many stories of his wealth, perhaps augmented by his squalid home and his tattered rags. Some summer people went out to see him saw wood one day, and one of them thought to test the old man's affluence by asking him to change a $100 bill. "Let me see it," said Ase. He looked at it carefully, and then reached into his rags, and he drew forth a roll of bills. He peeled off tens and fives rapidly and put the rest back in his pocket. The summer visitor counted his money and said, "There's only $90 here." The old man picked up his bucksaw and said, "I don't do business for nothing."

Speaking of horse hides makes me think of a young fellow who was well on the way to becoming a character in the fall with a few steeds of doubtful value. They are known as haying horses, because they can rake hay all right, but can't stand the heavy work of winter. Dealers like to get rid of such horses anyway they can in the fall, and they sometimes put them out on notes maturing the next May. If they haven't had any pay by May they repossess the horse and figure they were lucky to have him fed all winter.

During the World War horse hides went to an all-time top of $20. One young man used to come in every week with a horse hide and get his money. In the spring I heard

## QUEER CHARACTERS

the whole story. He'd take a haying horse on a note, claim he was going to yard some wood and he'd pay when he got the wood out. This left nearly every horse dealer in the county holding a note on a dead horse, and the total value of the notes was something like $6,000. I never knew that the young man killed the horses deliberately for their hides, but I suspect the worse.

One old outlaw in our neighborhood deserves recognition, if it's only here. He lived in a retired locality "that the foot of man never trod and the eye of God seldom saw." Every March the town meeting would put the town poor up at auction and knock them down to be boarded for the year by the lowest bidder. One year this old fellow bid in a poor case and got his money from the town up until November, when the pauper died. How to keep that poor money coming all winter was a problem for the old pirate, but he finally decided he would neglect to mention the demise of his charge to the town authorities. He carried the body up into the shed chamber and froze it. It kept nicely until March, and the benevolent old cuss collected board on it all winter.

A deformed character from a poor trash colony up back used to come in and trade with me. This colony was a degenerate lot who had intermarried and gone down the scale, and the old Jonas was about the worst of the bunch. He was about four feet tall, nearly as wide, and one story was that they used to yoke him in with a steer and use him for ploughing. One day the steer ran away, Jonas with him, and it took all the men to round them up. They finally cornered and attempted to unyoke the queer team. Jonas demonstrated he

## QUEER CHARACTERS

wasn't entirely lacking in sense when he yelled, "Unyoke the steer, unyoke the steer—I'll stand!"

One summer day some women went blueberrying up back, and they came running home with their pails half full and said a bear was stealing the lambs in the pasture. One of their men folks loaded his Queen's Arm with powder and shingle nails and struck up into the pasture. He found the bear, all right, making off with a bleating lamb. He drew a bead and pulled the trigger. The bear dropped the lamb, leaped a rod in the air, grabbed his posterior and began to swear in language that no bear is supposed to know about. It was Jonas robed in a bear skin out after a little fresh meat.

This colony recognized an old Uncle Dave and Aunt Matilda as king and queen. They would drive down to trade in a go-devil drawn by an aged white horse. A go-devil is a State of Maine vehicle—a single-horse sled with a pung body on it. It handles better in snow. One trip down someone fixed Uncle Dave up with some laughing water, and he and Aunt Matilda started home with the idea of consuming it on the way.

Aunt Matilda soon passed out, and Uncle Dave loaded her in the back of the pung with the grain and groceries. Uncle Dave continued to drink alone, and was pretty well jagged when the horse stopped at a depression in the road where the March sun had made a fairish puddle. The horse received a rather ponderous wallop from Uncle Dave's switch, gave a leap forward, and the old man plunged headfirst between the horse's heels and the crossbar. The horse went ahead far enough to drag Uncle Dave in the puddle and leave the load of grain, groceries, and Aunt Matilda over him.

## QUEER CHARACTERS

Neighboring farmers, hard at milking, came running at the screams of Uncle Dave and extricated him by tipping over the load. However, Aunt Matilda slept through the whole thing, and Uncle Dave wouldn't ever bring her to town again, said it wasn't safe.

One young chap in this colony used to come in and buy groceries, and when he told me one day he'd got married I gave him an aluminum teapot as a present. A short time later I saw his picture in the paper, and they had him down to the county seat to stand trial for murder. He had shot a neighbor. I followed the trial with interest, and it developed the neighbor used to come in of an evening to visit. He'd give the young man a quarter and a gallon jug and send him down to the road to buy a jug of cider. While the husband was gone on this errand the neighbor would solace himself with the company of the young wife.

Some of the neighbors put ideas in the young husband's head, so one night he went back and looked in the window and went and got his gun and shot the visitor. At the trial the lawyer built up quite a feeling of sympathy for the young man of inferior mentality—faced of a sudden with such a situation. He finally put the young man on the stand to tell his story, and he made a fine impression. At this point the judge asked, "If you get out of this scrape, what are you going to do?"

The young man said, "I'm going home and get three or four more." He got 20 years.

The country doctors have their own stories to tell, but the one we had there was timber for character material. He said the chief requirement for a doctor in Harmony was the ability

## QUEER CHARACTERS

to walk forty miles a day on snowshoes. The doctor is mentioned here because he was the one who finally shut up old Hosea Thomkins—our talkingest citizen. Hosea talked on every article in town meeting warrant, and nobody could seem to quiet him up. He would talk and talk and talk, nobody would listen, but he still talked. It spoiled town meeting for the rest of the voters.

After Hosea had delivered a long-winded speech one year, this doctor arose and spoke in his best professional manner. He said, "I have given long hours of study to Hosea's complaint and my diagnosis is that he is suffering from complete constipation of ideas accompanied by a violent diarrhea of conversation."

Hosea never spoke again in meeting, but one time he caught the doctor alone and behaved in such fashion that the doctor punched him in the nose and then treated him for his injuries. Hosea, unable to let well enough alone, had the doctor arrested and he was fined $5.

So the doctor sent Hosea a bill for $5 for fixing up his nose.

That's enough of characters—they circulate around the store all the time, and we finally forget they are characters at all. I told one of our best customers once, "You're the damnedest character in town, you ought to be in the movies."

He told me to look who's talking.

## 19

## GOD'S PEOPLE

Somewhere ages and ages hence, I may be sitting on a cloudbank in the comfort of the celestial scene, twanging sweet melody on a golden harp—but I doubt it. I have been described as a profane man, and on at least one memorable occasion as a godless man, but my chief trouble in matters sacred has been an inability to reconcile the dreams of the church members with life as I've come to know it. And I speak of this only because in my time I've done more than my share of contribution work to the upkeep of the churches.

The storekeeper gets stuck everytime he turns around—and the church is such a holy institution that no dictates of sound business principles can prevail. I've seen the time my books couldn't be balanced with all the cordwood in Somerset County, yet I'd shell out five dollars to help pay the minister in a church I never went to. The storekeeper is legal game in a perpetual open season for all the money-raising campaigns that go on. The churches are not the only offenders—the lodges and schools are as bad. Someone organizes a performance of a comic opera, and the storekeepers are practically blackmailed into paying for an ad that has no business value whatever.

But the churches always festered on me worst of all. Yet I do not consider myself particularly ungodly on account of it—but rather I think myself a little more than average faithful because of my contributions and look to my feelings as the net profit. If it pleases me to grumble, I've paid for the right.

One of my earliest memories is of a religious experience. Just what it did for me has never been openly manifest, but it was an experience calling for much faith—and I was let down. Father left me to saw wood while he went away on business, and made it understood that I was not to dillydally by sliding on the hills with worthless friends who had nothing better to do.

I sawed a while, but the boys and girls on the hill joyfully called amongst themselves and seemed to be having such a fine time that I was tempted. I reflected on what father would do to me when he came home if the pile wasn't sawed, and then I would hear the boys and girls, and I finally succumbed. I got out our old pung, pulled it over to the hill, and invited everyone to ride. I sat on a sled between the shafts and steered the pung down the hill.

The boys and girls pronounced this a great improvement, and we had several rides. Then one of the girls wanted to steer, and again I succumbed. She got flustered and dropped the shafts just when the speed was most fun. One of them snapped off.

I never felt that way before. Doom, without the slightest

## GOD'S PEOPLE

question, was about to descend on me. Father would lick me for not sawing wood. He would lick me for going sliding. Then the pung! He had bought it at an auction for thirty-five cents and was most proud of it. He would lick me for breaking the pung. There was no pleasure within me. I was undone.

We sneaked the pung back in the barn and then the boys and girls went home and left me to my sorrow. I climbed up into the mow, walked out on the big beam, and dangled my legs into a space that was shallow compared to the depths of my despair. I reflected to learn if any remedy might prevail. I appealed to the Providence of whom my mother had taught. And Providence, at this point, aided me.

Father was working with his wood team—six cattle in three yokes in a string. He had two yokes of two or three years, and an old team on the tongue. The old team was a bull and an ox. The ox was bigger, but the bull was so much more powerful that the clevis in his yoke was set off-center an inch and a half. He was a frightening bull for all the world but father. Mother worried herself sick, but father worked with the snorting and headshaking bull as if he were another docile ox. That morning, when father walked the six cattle out of the yard, the bull had put on an exhibition. Mother watched from the door and said, "Sure as you're born, that bull will kill your father some day."

I had been taught to pray for help if I needed it. If the bull was going to kill father, I felt now was the time. I climbed down off the beams, slid down the mow, discreetly, went in behind the mowing machine and knelt down. Very earnestly I prayed that the bull would kill father before he got home. I cast my burden on the Lord, and as soon as I stood up I felt much better.

I went back to sawing wood, and kept one eye on the road. Far off on the rim of the world I saw the team appear at last—and father was teaming the cattle along in his usual good health. The team came down Hall's Hill and disappeared behind Frazier's Hill. I sawed some more wood. It would happen, I figure, behind Frazier's Hill. But then the team came up over Frazier's Hill and father was still teaming them. I watched the load crawl nearer and nearer. The Lord was unnecessarily slow, I thought. He had still withheld His hand when father turned the load into the yard and stopped the steers by the woodpile.

"You'll have to unyoke the oxen," he said. "My head aches so I can hardly see." Then I saw that God moves in a mysterious way His wonders to perform. If He thought it best to kill father with a headache instead of by means of the bull—the matter was out of my hands now. I was reconciled, and no longer feared for my hide.

But this powerful religious experience soured on me when I discovered that the real solution took exceedingly small help from divine power. My uncle came home that night after long years in the West, and everyone was so glad to see him father never thought about my woodpile. The next day Uncle wanted to use the pung, and when he found a broken shaft he made a new one with a maple sapling and a drawshave—and in a matter of minutes he was off behind the mare to get his trunk at the Falls. No one has asked me to this day how the shaft got broken.

The incident, however, has been recalled many times since,

## GOD'S PEOPLE

and while I am frequently ashamed that I had too little sense to think of making a new shaft myself, I have also reflected that the Creator has more brains than I have anyway—and I'm willing to leave everything to Him. It seems to me that if a little boy's plight requires heavenly interference, it isn't necessary for the little boy to bother reminding Him about it. Spiritually, I have since followed such a belief, partly because my observations have never suggested a better.

I have, however, given the churches in my community a good chance. I was brought up by a pious mother who indoctrinated me after the custom of the time and remarked occasionally that I was to go into the ministry. But as I grew older I found my business required me to get along with people, and this included God's people as well as the rest of us.

The average country minister has struck me as a poor sort of contributor to the social scene. Someone asked me once what I thought of God. I said God seemed like a nice enough chap, but I was surprised anyone in his position hired so much cheap help. And I have always thought God's people ought to stack up a little better than the ordinary non-church member—and I haven't found that so.

I draw no hard and fast line—many sincere worshippers of God are above my opinions and have no need of them. There are many earnest followers of the meek and lowly Jesus but these same people are the meek kind and they get an awful pushing around from the other class and have very little to do with church business. The ones of which I complain are the Old Hardened Christians—they run the church and bring a quart of skimmed milk to the church supper and take home a basket full of pies and cakes and other provisions. They

## GOD'S PEOPLE

censor the morals of the community and interfere in other people's business and expect to get a front seat at heaven. If I ever go to hell, as they have told me many times I must, I shall certainly get a lot of comfort out of meeting some of these deluded people. For I think they will be there too, because I can't believe they have fooled the Almighty that much.

When I first located in Harmony I was approached by a committee to see if I wouldn't subscribe to the minister's salary. They showed me a paper, and about everyone in town was on it. My competitor, who was a leader in that particular church, was at the head of the list and I matched him, although I didn't feel I could afford it. The next winter the minister told me he couldn't get a cent of his salary. I had paid mine, and I asked about the others and found out how such things work. The previous minister had gone away leaving a few bills, and the subscription had been to take care of the amount. The new minister hadn't seen any of it. The poor devil was actually needy, and I marveled at his stubbornness in trying to spread the gospel among sinners who would pull such a trick.

About that time we were called together to organize a Red Cross drive. Up in the front row was a good sister who had been active in getting the pastor's back bills paid. She said, "It is useless to expect us to give more. We have impoverished ourselves this year to support the church." We less pious townsmen who felt less limited gave the Red Cross a good send-off according to our means or meanness, and when the meeting was over I bottonholed the church treasurer.

## GOD'S PEOPLE

"How much," I asked, "does it take to impoverish the Joneses?"

He looked at me candidly and snapped, "Two dollars."

Now these people owned their own home in a prosperous small town. They had received one legacy of $5,000 that we all knew about. The old man had a pension of $50 a month, and the lady did nursing for those who would pay her price—which was higher than the usual. I don't believe they ever spent half the old man's pension. They rented the other half of their house to an unbeliever who said he could always tell when the Methodists were going to have a supper, because that was the time he couldn't find any eggs in his hen house. Sister Jones always baked a cake.

Yet Sister Jones was a self-appointed censor of everything in town, and glazed all her activities with a church-going shine. To my mind she was essentially immoral. She was always worrying because someone else might do something naughty. Once she told me the Grange Dances on Friday night were demoralizing the community—our young people were being ruined. I always liked the Grange, and figure it's done at least as much good as some churches.

So I told Sister Jones we had one thing far worse than the Grange Dances. "What?" she said with a glitter in her eyes. It startled her that something wicked was going on and she didn't know about it.

"Wednesday night prayer meetings," I said. She was horrified and said so.

"Our young people go to a Grange time," I said, "and then they go home. They go to a prayer meeting, which lets out at 7:30, and they don't go home afterward. If you want

## GOD'S PEOPLE

to know where they go—take a look in my ice house, or on the freight platform behind the store. I learned about life by watching prayer meeting products through my back window."

Sister Jones was even more horrified. She whirled and went out, and it came to me that she frequently mentioned me as an influence for evil in the town. Yet for years I helped support the church that she employed to rate her position in the community. However, when the influenza epidemic struck our little town and laid so many of us low, I couldn't help noticing the sparing manner in which the devoted followers of organized religion helped out. One minister went home to his people. One openly refused to preach committal sermons for those who died of influenza.

One little divinity student who was out in the woods gaining experience stuck with me—I always figured he hadn't yet gained enough experience to know how a church person acts. When it was over we had buried 40 in our little community—and we gave the righteous and unrighteous exactly the same treatment. The divinity student and I never had a sick day. Perhaps the student prayed a little, but I relied wholly on God's good sense. Perhaps He spared the divinity student for the same reason—but I've always suspected the other two ministers, who had always a lot to say about the glories of Paradise, must have been a little faint-hearted at their chances of making the grade.

My innermost reflections about the nature of salvation are pertinent here only because the poor country storekeeper finds so much of his profit tied up in supporting the churches. Not his own church, but all of them. In comes a committee seeking donations to pay the coal bill. Who can say no to a

## GOD'S PEOPLE

church? Who would say it, whether any business considerations are involved or not? So we shell out, and I think most of us come to regard the religiously inclined as a burden to the man who wants to make an honest living in trade.

I daresay that throughout the years I've been in business, I've paid more than the pious for the support of the churches —all the churches—in my communities. Not only that, but any storekeeper carries on his books the evidence of charities that are never sanctified by the aura of the church. I've seen good church members going hungry—including some minister's families—and have solemnly invoked damnation on all the Sister Joneses in town for not going to their aid. Some of these people got onto my books, and some of them are still in arrears.

Anyway, it always roiled me when sanctimonious church members came into the store and took me to task because I didn't tend out more faithfully at morning worship. I usually remarked that I had been driven away from church by poor preaching. I always sat in the pew and thought how much better I could do it. Once I gave in, and agreed to attend a sermon on Character Building. The music was pretty, and I heard the minister read the chapter about Elijah and the Priests of Baal. I sat as at an interesting play and heard that great story again. I thought to myself: "What a chance to draw a comparison between the character of Elijah and of the King's servant who played both ends against the middle!" But the sermon!

The preacher drew our attention to the twelve stones of the altar, then the twelve tribes of Israel, and the twelve months of the year, and the twelve signs of the zodiac, and

## GOD'S PEOPLE

the twelve Apostles, and the twelve great planets—and by that time I was ready to go home and conduct my own services in the relative calm of my own reflection. I did. I went home and read that story again, and dwelt on it to my own satisfaction.

About all that it ever came to was a decision to keep on supporting the churches on condition they leave me to my own salvation. Anyway, so it was that I was accused by a visiting committee, seeking a donation for another minister's salary, of being a godless man. They told me sincerely that I would roast eternally in hell, and indicated that my plight would have their utmost approbation.

Well, I know something about that. When I was a boy I had to pump water for our cattle. Some people had a new-fangled cucumber pump, but father stuck to the old chain pump. The chain pump was one of the milestones on mankind's thirsty road of progress. The old well where Rebekah got the water for Eleazar had projecting rocks that one climbed down with a jug. Later someone thought of a rope and a bucket, and then along came the well sweep. Then, I guess, came the chain pump. An endless chain, with cups on it, was turned by a crank and a sprocket at the top, and it passed under a pulley below the water. On the way down the chain ran free, but on the way up it moved through a wooden spout and brought up water. The pump, as I've described it, lacked only a motor. At nine years of age, I was the motor.

The well was located on a knoll directly in the wind and between the house and the barn. Usually the old wells were located in a depression so the barn drainage would run into

## GOD'S PEOPLE

them, but grandmother was fussy, and she located this one. I would take my stance at the pump once a day, collect my gumption, and commence to crank. The chain would clank, the little washer-cups would come bounding up out of the spout, and soon the water would trickle from the hole. A V-shaped trough led the water to a huge tub hollowed from a punkin'-pine log, around which clustered the thirstiest animals ever assembled in one place, a flock of camels to the contrary notwithstanding.

I became proficient at pumping just enough. When the animals had finished there was little water to be drawn out of the tub against freezing. From October to April this job was performed in a bleakness and frigidity that I can neither describe nor people would readily believe. When I went away from home every job I encountered was pleasant compared with cranking that old chain pump.

And I believe theologians make their mistake when they threaten me with the fires of hell. I have seen 40 below zero too often to be afraid of a seat near the fire. But if someone could convince me that my present mode of life would put me in danger of having to stand at the northwest corner of our old barn in a continuous January and pump water with our old chain pump for twenty-seven sheep, ten cattle, and three horses throughout eternity, I am sure I would make a strenuous effort to live a better life.

## 20

## GRANGERS

After delivering myself so testily about the church people, I can find something good to say about another phase of community life—the secret orders. They, too, come around once in a while for an ad in a program, and they sometimes want a discount on groceries for their lodge suppers—but they are loyal. I've found if I'm kind to a Knight of Pythias, the brotherhood usually reciprocates. I've joined some of the orders, and among their respective mysteries is found the reasons—these societies mean something to those within them. In the small town in Maine, however, one fraternity always stands out above the others from the country storekeeper's point of view—the Grange.

Founded upon the moralities of agriculture, with the changing seasons depicted didactically for the assembled members, the Grange offers the rural family a chance to participate on equal footing in a program of mystery, education, entertainment, refreshment, and (although not publicly acknowledged) politics. The children as well as the parents

# GRANGERS

attend, and to be a Granger is at one time a distinction and no distinction at all. This paradox arises from the fact that almost everyone throughout the countryside belongs.

I first joined the Grange when I was living at Lisbon, after I left the Portsmouth store because of my health. I always had a flair for talking on my feet, and memorizing the ritual was no great task. I served Pine Tree Grange as master, and helped out in other stations until I could handle any portion of the Grange work. This, of course, made me well known among the membership, and I was soon to find out it gave me an open door into many situations. Acquaintanceships ripened into friendships, and I found the Grange a great help in doing business. Naturally, one of the aspects of this business was a brotherly consideration of those with whom I did it, and on such spirit is the Grange built. Whatever town I found myself in, the password of the Grange was all I needed to found lasting friendships, and in the meetings it was always easy for me to arise and relate some little anecdote.

When I got into the store again, the Grange was a big help in bringing friends into the store. A trade is a trade, and Grangers knew that as well as I—so we moved along together in good fellowship, and I always considered the Grange a business asset as well as an excellent place to indulge in community betterment.

I wandered into a strange town one afternoon, and found the Grange was meeting for an all day session. The state lecturer was to speak, and when the local lecturer recognized me she asked me to say a few words. I told her I had to catch the 3:15 train, but she said she'd take care of that, and she cautioned the state lecturer that he had to finish so I could speak and still catch that train.

I cast about for a few things to say, and listened to the speaker. He was a little man and he talked on and on, and left me very little time. I took the floor and commended his remarks. "We can all profit by his fine words," I said, "but his talk reminds me of a woman down home who went up to Auburn to visit her daughter. The daughter met her at the train, and as they were walking out to the house they went by a fire and a fire engine pumping water on it. The old lady watched the engine with breathless interest, and clasped her daughter's arm with the remark, "Who in the world would think that little thing could hold so much?"

I raced out of the hall after the train, and the shrieks and screams that pursued me down the stairs made me think some others thought about the same as I did.

Long-winded talkers in the Grange are at a discount, but good stories are always appreciated, and I made it a practice always to have one worth telling. At Harmony I found the ladies liked one now and then with some spice in it, and I tried to oblige them. This led to the situation in which I *had* to have a story. One evening I arrived late to meeting, and had to wait while the secret opening was taken care of behind locked doors. Out in the hall a group of women greeted me and asked what my story was going to be.

I told them the only story I had was a little off-color, but they insisted they could handle it, and I related the following:

## GRANGERS

"A colored girl with three children was riding on a trolley when another colored girl got on and greeted her happily. 'Why,' she said, 'I ain't seen you in the longest time—and you married with three children! Land sakes!' The other girl said, 'Yes, I has three children, but I ain't married.' Alarmed at uncovering such a condition, the second girl proceeded to inquire what the children were named. 'Well,' said Mandy, 'I call this first one Ignorance, I call this second one Carelessness, and the last one is just Hard Luck.'"

The ladies shrieked with joy, and as soon as the meeting gave them a chance they peddled the story to all and sundry. The lull between the business session and the work of the evening was all they needed to convey my story to everyone present. About that time the Master came to me and said I would have to take the part of the Assistant Steward, as that officer wasn't present. I could fill in anywhere, so I put on the regalia of my station and waited for the meeting to resume.

The Assistant Steward takes up the password, and at the proper time conducts the candidate through the initiation ceremony. At the proper time I repaired to the anteroom and found a candidate—an old maid schoolma'am. She was about forty years old and not at all attractive. She had a little wad of hair about the color of last year's June grass, and her hair sprung away from this to form scolding-locks all down her neck. Her glasses were thick, and she looked as if she expected the worst and was steeled to meet it.

All in the best form I started her around the hall and the initiation began. Soon we came to an officer who undertakes to discourage the candidate, and magnifies the dangers. He recites a paragraph intended to induce the victim to go no farther, but to turn back and be safe. At this point, it was my part to say, "The person who has just addressed you is Ignorance, accompanied by his companions, Sloth and Superstition. Heed him not if you hope to advance."

I saw at once that I'd never have such a chance again, and in my most solemn manner I warned the candidate against listening to Ignorance, Carelessness, and Hard Luck. The roar that burst from the crowd nearly swept the teacher off her feet. The two hundred people present quieted down after a bit, and then someone would snicker, some old farmer would burst out with a loud "Haw Haw!" and off they would go again. I've always wondered if the old maid ever heard the story, or if she just thought we were crazy.

I liked the Grange, always did my part in the work gladly and with what I considered ability—and I found it well worth my while both in fellowship and in business. I journeyed often to neighboring towns and took part in their Grange programs, until I was as well known throughout my territory as the mailmen. Up in Cambridge was a little Grange where we used to have some mighty fine times, and I made the acquaintance of Ed Randall who bought everything he needed at my store for years and years.

One day Ed was in the store trading, and he said the Grange was having a contest—two teams were lined up and each was trying to outdo the other at story telling. Three members were judges, and at each meeting they evaluated the stories and kept score. At the end of the contest the losers

## GRANGERS

had to feed the winners. Ed said, "Tell me a story I can use to put my side ahead."

I fixed him up as best I could, and he opined that it was risky. His wife was captain of his team, and if the Grangers didn't blacklist him on account of the story, his wife would kill him if he ever told it. I bolstered him, claiming almost everything would go at Grange, and people weren't as offendable as he thought. This convinced him, and next meeting the Lecturer announced, "Next will be a story by Ed." Ed told the story I gave him:

> "A young lady school teacher was leading her class through 'prosody or the art of versification.' She said, 'Now, children, I want each of you to compose a rhyme and bring it to class tomorrow.' The next day the children read off their poems, and they finally came to Johnny. Johnny got up and read:
>
>> 'I sat within a shady nook,
>> Beside a little babbling brook,
>> And watched a pretty little lass
>> Wade in the water clear up to her knees.'
>
> The teacher said, 'Yes, Johnny, but the last line doesn't rhyme.' Johnny said, 'I know it, but it would have if we hadn't had so much dry weather this fall.'"

Ed reported afterward that his story got the highest award of all those in the contest, that his wife looked daggers but touched him not, and he felt his popularity in Cambridge went up about five notches.

The Grange isn't all story telling, however. Their literary

programs bring a form of much needed education to people who are otherwise without it. The state officers who visit around bring in much of news and opinion, and as a common meeting ground for people with common problems and interests it can't be beaten. And as far as Maine is concerned, it's no secret that political fortunes have gained and waned according as Grangers decided pro or con. I always felt the Grange membership was well worth while, and I could have got along if non-Grangers never came near my place.

## 21

## UNDERTAKING

MORTICIANS, they call them today—but as far as I am concerned the license called me an embalmer and the folks in Harmony called me the undertaker. I got to be an undertaker the same way I went into handling hay—there looked to be a penny in it, and I have never been downright opposed to making money.

One day I was cost-marking a shipment of shoes and I heard activity upstairs where for some time there had been no activity at all. I learned a young man from a neighboring town was opening a funeral business with furniture as a sideline. He had worked with his father, but they had a fight, and he struck out on his own.

I watched him for a while, and although I never had any desire to get into that line of business, it did occur to me that his profession was seemingly profitable, and he appeared to have all kinds of money without doing much to get it. One day he and his old man made up, and he left town. I bought him out. At that time I knew nothing whatever about the

## UNDERTAKING

business, except that a fellow up on the back road charged two dollars to dig the hole.

I had a man who had conducted funerals, and I didn't pay much attention during the fall rush, but after things quieted down and winter set in I decided to get me a license. I found a course at a school of anatomy and embalming was essential. Mostly because I was afraid I'd lose my man and be stuck high and dry, I made my choice. I went to Boston one night on the train, and the next morning I called up a school I found listed in the directory and said I wanted to be an undertaker. They told me the course cost $50, and took three months, and to be on hand Friday morning at 9:30. I was there, and found a new class about to take up their studies.

I introduced myself to the dean and said, "I'm in a hurry, I can't spend three months." He said he could give it as fast as I could take it, and he started the first lecture. A number of students, all much younger than myself, asked questions—especially how to spell words—but I didn't open my head. When the lecture was about half-finished the dean stopped and said to me, "Let me see your notes." He looked at them for several minutes and asked, "Where did you learn to write like that?"

I said, "Taking grocery orders over the phone." He said, "You won't be here long." And I wasn't. At eleven o'clock he dismissed the class, but told me to stick around and he'd give me another lecture. He gave me two. That afternoon he gave me another—and then we went out on a demonstration. A man had died in an insane asylum, had been post-mortemed and thrown together before being shipped to his people. We had a lot of work to do on him. I had to raise the femoral

## UNDERTAKING

artery, and kept telling myself it was a lot like drawing a hen. I had seen charts at the school, and with good luck I did it all right. The dean claimed I must have seen it done before.

The next day I got more lectures, and on Sunday I read over my book of notes and looked at the charts. Monday came a quiz, and after a time the dean told me not to answer the questions, but to sit back and listen, and he wanted to see me first thing in the morning. Tuesday he said, "Now you don't have to stay any longer—I'll send some charts and books you can study, so you go home to your business and bone up for the state examinations. I'll send you questions they've asked at former exams, and you'll be all right."

So I went home, having studied embalming from a Friday to a Tuesday and spent $71.80 including my railroad ticket. At the state examinations I was naturally nervous. The inadequacy of my education seemed extensive. Of the forty-eight questions, thirty-six had to be answered correctly. The dean of the school had asked me to get a set of the exam question for his students, but as they wouldn't give me extra copies, I made a copy as I went along and put it in my pocket. I finished the questions in no time, half-sure my answers couldn't be right because they were so easy. I was the first one up, and I handed the secretary my paper with an uneasy smile. He smiled back and asked if it had been hard. I said, "Only one question bothered me, number five—What is a Viscus?"

He said, "You know what viscera are? Well, that is the plural form." He handed back the paper, and I added that to give me a perfect score. I sent the questions and my answers to the dean, and he wrote that he had made them the official

## UNDERTAKING

answers for the school. Thus I became an undertaker, and I operated as such as long as I stayed in Harmony.

I write this because at heart I am a rebel. I regard the entire as an attempt to sew up the extremely profitable undertaking business for "Me and my wife, my son John and his wife, us four and no more." The questions they asked me had very little to do with the business of preparing bodies for burial and safeguarding the public health. They merely make it hard for outsiders to get in. To get the license I had, a man must now have a high school education and have worked two years with a licensed embalmer, besides attending an approved school for six months at a fee of at least $500. He can't take the state examination without this. Yet he is in the end no more legally qualified than I was. He may have more of a bedside manner, more spit and polish, more tactful methods of dealing with the bereaved—but I don't think he has any more concrete knowledge of the basic duties than I have.

I find most people think undertaking is a depressing business. Death is dreaded by nearly all of us. I thought the business would seem so to me. I found out the opposite is true. To my surprise I found the undertaker is a very welcome guest in most homes. The old folks who pass away have generally worn out their welcome and usually they are glad to move on too. No one says so, but you see signs of relief on all faces. The face of a person dying merely from old age is usually a peaceful face. Death is not a bad friend to old folks. Of course, there are young people who die, and then I am sorry. A child, a young mother, a happy father—when these died I was filled with sorrow for days. Undertaking was a business—but it made me philosophize at times. I never

## UNDERTAKING

answered any of the queries I raised about the reasons. I don't know why young and happy people die.

But while I never got over being sad at some cases, most cases came and went without particular emotion from me. In the beginning I had hard work to charge $65 for a casket and box that cost $9, with a lining and handles that cost $1.50. But as time went on I went out gaily for the $250 jobs that didn't set me back as much as you might think.

The dean at the school told me a lot depended on getting a good start. A young student in South Boston got a good start by selling a $1,250 bronze casket which cost him $450. Then he persuaded the family on a cremation, and by giving the crematory man $10 he got the casket back again. He sold it five times before the widow involved in the last sale decided a good, old-fashioned interment was good enough for her dead. There are sad moments for all of us, and no doubt this was one for him—but he did get a good start from it.

I had just lettered "Licensed Embalmer" under the other letters on my store window when a man came in and said, "Father is dead, I'd like you to look after him." We picked out a casket, discussed details, and I drove up to lay out the body. The old man was ninety years old, and had contemplated his death with calmness. He had asked for a Baptist minister, and that was something we didn't have at that time. We did, however, have the promise of a student to get experience, and he was due up on the train the morning of the funeral. That morning I went up in the country, to the remote section where the old man had lived, and set up the casket in the rough and almost bare home. Then I hurried back to Harmony to meet the train.

## UNDERTAKING

The student minister was a frightened-looking young man, but with him he had the best-looking girl friend I ever saw anyone sporting. They got off the train with the Spirit of the Lord upon them and looked about at the wild and remote community they had been called upon to serve. The girl was planning to go right back on the train, but she decided to go to the funeral.

I asked the lad, "Have you ever had a call to preach the gospel to the heathen?" He allowed he never had. "Then you have now." I told him he had to go back into the country with me and help bury a patriarch. He was visibly unnerved, but he seen his duty and he done it. The girl came along to steady him, and she turned out to be a grand person to have along on such an expedition. She offered to sing, if the family wished.

When we arrived at the house we found the whole countryside present. Countryfolk love funerals. We had to tear some boards off the fence and saw blocks off some logs to make benches. Then we found a box for the preacher, and I was ready to give him the highball when a daughter beckoned me into the kitchen. She said her father had always liked a certain record on the phonograph, and she produced a disk and pointed at the phonograph in the front room. The services began.

I'll hand it to the young man. He did a bang-up job and had the mourners right out straight. I didn't know what was coming when, at the proper time, I slipped the battered record on the phonograph and set down the needle. But it wasn't as bad as all that. It was, *When the Roll Is Called Up Yonder, I'll Be There*. Some of the old-timers wept, and I

## UNDERTAKING

remember I was glad to have pleased them. Then the minister offered a prayer, and the young lady sang *Nearer, My God, to Thee* in the most beautiful voice I've ever heard. There wasn't a dry eye in the house. We lifted the casket into the old Democrat wagon, and drove the old man to the cemetery where we left him with eternity.

The three of us were silent on the way back to Harmony. The sky was clear, the mountain scenery was lovely. As we drove down into town the evening train was making up, and we put the girl on it. She was a secretary to a city insurance firm, and had never been in the country before. She looked up at the hills before getting on the train. When she said good-bye to me she said, "I've never had such a lovely day in my life before—it's been gorgeous."

Anyway, that was my start. It naturally impressed me full as much as it did the young lady, but I know now it was purely routine business! In our out-of-the-way town we were sometimes without a physician, which complicated the business somewhat. However, we had an automobile mechanic who had studied medicine two years, and although he had no license and couldn't charge for his services he sometimes had quite a practice going. He was better than some doctors we had, and often more communicative to me. Once he helped me out of a delicate situation.

A man came in and said his wife's brother was dead up at his house. He said to make all the arrangements and he'd pay the bill. That pleased me—we always like to find the responsible party first. I asked if they wanted a funeral at the home. He said, "Hell, no—get him out of my place as quick's God'll let you!"

## UNDERTAKING

It seemed the deceased was a black sheep and had just got out of state prison in a neighboring state. He sneaked into his brother's house, got into bed before they could kick him out and died there. I asked the brother where I should take the body. He said, "I don't give a damn—just so's you get him to hell out of my place. He's been there too long now."

When I got to the house the auto-mechanic-physician was there and I asked to see the death certificate. The cause of death was given as "acute yellow atrophy of the liver." This was a new one on me, and I asked him what it was. He said, "Oh, that's something you put down when you don't know what it is." That made me remember the embalming school dean's remark, "Autopsies at the Bellevue Hospital reveal the diagnosis was wrong in 66⅔ percent of the cases. Your guess is as good as the doctor's."

I decided acute yellow atrophy of the liver, in this case, was a condition not unknown in some state prisons, and to a competent physician it has another name. Anyway we lowered the deceased down from his attic room through a scuttle, dressed him, and took him to church. A few curious came to the obsequies and numerous relatives. The minister preached an eloquent sermon about the glories God has prepared for those who love Him. I told him he would go far as a diplomat, and he said, "What else could I say?"

Being the only undertaker in town, and the town serving a wide section, gave me considerable business in this field. I won't say I enjoyed it, but I did consider it a worthy addition to the grocery and sundry business. Undertaking moves in orderly fashion and everything is under control until an epidemic strikes. With me it was the influenza in 1918. At the

## UNDERTAKING

time we had good country physician service, but the disease was new to them and they tried to treat it like pneumonia. Government physicians came in to instruct them, but by that time I had buried forty members of our little town. It was a heartbreaking time for everyone—fully as much so for me. I had become professional with the ordinary routine—but this was too much. When the epidemic subsided I found my wife was looking more tired and drawn than seemed called for even by that ordeal, and I tore out to find one of the government doctors who was in town.

He gave us the news straight. One lung was gone, the other affected. She might live a year in this climate. I sold out lock, stock, and barrel in a matter of hours, and we went to the mountains of North Carolina in a matter of days. She lived less than a year.

## 22

### CORN BREAD, ETC.

THE winter I was in North Carolina I collected the material for a book I planned to write on southern cooking. The book has two chapters in it, as follows:

#### Chap. I

There is nothing in the South fit for a Yankee to eat.

#### Chap. II

If there were, nobody down there knows how to cook it.

I have taken a keen interest in the art of cooking since I sat on the pantry shelf and helped mother roll molasses cookies—with the handle on the pump prodding me in the back. The so-called good old days were days of good eating—and I enjoyed that aspect of them very much. Yet we spent very little for food. The quality of our table depended partly on the produce of the farm, but more so on the skill with which mother and grandmother blended and arranged their

## CORN BREAD, ETC.

ingredients. They used what they had, and made everything count. We ate cheaply, but the food was touched by genius in the kitchen.

Perhaps that is the reason things taste differently today. But we must have good cooks somewhere, and I'm willing to admit many of the goods in my store have not been made better by modern improvements. I regard the eat-for-health advocates as beneath my notice. They are all full of vitamins and minerals and are happy in their state. I care not for them. I hold to an older philosophy which tells me things good to eat ought, also, to taste good. Perhaps they are injurious in their indigestibility. I hope once more before I die I can undermine my health with some of the foods we can't get because somebody says they aren't good for us.

I have sold a good many products I have been ashamed of—fine-ground corn meal, sulphur-dioxide molasses, packaged coffee, all manner of things my grandmother would have turned up her nose at clear back to here. We folks were brought up on a homespun cookery formula that has no equal elsewhere in the world. We may be cranks on it, but it has its faithful adherents. Progress and the advertising business have taken some of our most needed ingredients away from us.

Such as corn meal. In the back shed we had a meal chest—rye meal in one end, and over the partition corn meal. Corn was harvested, traced, and hung on the big beams in the attic of the old farmhouse. One day grandmother would come down and opine the corn was dry enough to grind. Home from the old Holmes & Blanchard stone mill, the meal was coarse. We always had rye ground at the same time. And

## CORN BREAD, ETC.

after the day at the mill, we had corn bread of such quality my mouth drips as I recall it.

Once I was traveling in New Hampshire and stopped overnight at a farmhouse. The woman apologized at breakfast. She said, "I've just got johnnycake for breakfast." I said, "Have you got enough?" I'd rather have johnnycake than a license to steal. After breakfast I asked for her receipt, and it was the same as my grandmother used:

> Two cups Indian meal, one cup flour, two cups sweet milk, one cup sour, spoonful salt and soda, half cup of molasses. If you haven't sour milk, use sweet and two spoonfuls of cream of tartar.

If you haven't an old-fashioned family, cut this down as it makes about half an acre. If you want it extra rich and short, grind up a cup of suet and mix it in. This isn't quite so hard on butter. There should be a law to hang people getting caught putting eggs or sugar in corn bread. I will furnish the rope if they'll hang them in my yard so I can enjoy the spectacle.

But why bother? The basic ingredient—good corn meal—is a thing of the past. Corn meal today is bolted within an inch of its life, and the modern generation is deprived of this preview of heaven. They know nothing about rye-and-Indian bread with baked beans on Saturday night, about Indian pudding baked in a tall crock with raisins in it. I haven't had decent corn meal in my store for years.

Or dry beans. Where can I buy a barrel of Jacob's cattle beans? You don't know them? The Bible says Jacob's cattle were ring-streaked and speckled. So were the beans. Once in

## CORN BREAD, ETC.

a while a farmer brings in a bag of them, and I almost fling myself in his arms. Sell them? I sell only those that are left after I fill the can in my kitchen.

Or molasses. Molasses used to be a big item. In the old days we'd have a hogshead coming, and people would bring in their jugs before it arrived. The jugs were smeared and smooched around the mouths from years of use, and each had a string to the handle with a carrying stick through it. When the hogshead came we'd tap it, and one man would draw until all the jugs were full. The next day everyone would have new molasses for receipts that are, today, pretty much forgotten as hogsheads.

Those old molasses hogsheads came up by boat to Portland. We thought Puerto Rican molasses the best product— we'd read Mayagüez or Ponce on the heads, two ports where ships were loaded. The sugar would settle in the hogsheads, and after we'd drawn out all the molasses some farmer would dicker for the hogshead. They used them for watering tubs, and by sawing a hogshead in two at the bung they'd get a pair of nice drinking tubs for cattle. But we knew they were also after the sugar. We'd sell the hogsheads for about a dollar, and sometimes the farmer would get a washtub full of sugar. His wife would purify it and get a good grade of molasses from it, and we would notice that the family didn't bring their jug in for a long time. My father used to buy the things, and after he got the sugar out he'd sell the tubs for more than the hogshead cost.

People say molasses isn't as good as it used to be. It isn't. The present generation can't tell good molasses anyway, and will pay the price for poor stuff. The vacuum pans and cen-

## CORN BREAD, ETC.

trifugal separators used in the modern sugar plants extract the last ounce of sugar, and the gelatinous product that remains hasn't much authority as molasses. In Barbados they are still old fashioned, and there they grind the cane and make the whole thing into molasses. Barbados molasses is about the only decent one on the market today—and that is hard to get. Even that is shipped in huge tanks, and when the tanks are drained they squirt in live steam and melt the settled sugar, whereupon they have more molasses. One or two companies still handle a molasses that isn't treated with sulphur-dioxide—and consequently will stand up under the brisk treatment of a good cook.

It takes the old-fashioned kind to pull into taffy, to make molasses sauce for steamed pudding, or to give that zip to molasses apple pie, cake, or doughnuts. Don't come to my store looking for good molasses—and if you know of a place where it can be had, wait and I'll go with you. It isn't the storekeeper's fault. It's modern methods and the milk-toast public who will put up with it.

One time a boy with his mouth open came into the store and said, "Mother wants two quarts of molasses." He held out a tin pail. I pumped two quarts in the pail and he started out with it. I said, "Hold on, son, where's your money?" He looked at me as blank as a washboard and said, "In the pail." Good-bye quarter.

I suppose the best object lesson in this sort of thing lies in the coffee situation. I suppose the most hot air we've seen since Nero burned Rome is to be found in coffee advertising. They've shot the works, and the public has swallowed the whole story to the last drop.

## CORN BREAD, ETC.

I know of a chain store that displayed seven kinds of coffee with prices from thirteen to thirty-eight cents a pound—and the man who managed the store told me a truck brought one sack of coffee every morning and they filled all the bins from it. The people who bought the thirty-eight-cent coffee turned up their noses at the cheap trash who would be contented with the thirteen-cent kind.

Well, I know that sort of thing will work. In Portsmouth we sold three kinds of port wine—California Port, Tarragona Port, and Douro Port, priced at twenty-five cents, fifty cents, and one dollar a pint. I bought the three wines by dropping a card to a wholesaler in Boston, and down would come three kegs. One day a little Jew came in and said he represented the San Gabriel Wine Co., and claimed he had a port better than anything we had in stock for twenty-seven cents a gallon F.O.B. New York. I bought a barrel, and when it came I examined it and shrugged my shoulders. It was all one to me. I filled the three kegs from it, and we still sold three kinds of wine—when we sold the twenty-seven-cent-a-gallon stuff for a dollar a pint it didn't hurt us any to speak of.

One day a woman came in looking for port wine. She had a sick woman under her care and the doctor had prescribed wine. She had been paying $1.50 to a competitor for a bottle holding a pint and a half, and she thought maybe she could do better. I said, "Mrs. Hanan, I'm going to put you up three samples. These are all California wines, and I think the best is as good as any. You try them out, and decide which is the best. They'll cost you twenty-five cents, fifty cents, and one dollar a quart. The cheap one I just put in for comparison, but the fifty-cent one is a good, sound wine, and I think it is

SAN
GABRI
CALIFORNIA
TARRAGONNA
PORT
DUORO
PORT
XX
STEPHEN J.
VOORHIES

## CORN BREAD, ETC.

just what you need. The dollar one may be a better flavor because of its age, but I don't feel it's worth the difference to you."

She came back and said she had a surgeon in the Navy Yard, who was a thorough chemist and a good judge of wines, try them out. He told her the dollar wine was as good as any he'd seen, the fifty-cent wine was suitable for her needs but lacked flavor, while the twenty-five cent wine was perfectly vile and there ought to be a law against selling it. We continued selling three kinds of wine at three prices—and it all came out of one barrel. I took it out myself.

That's the way with coffee. Some years ago the Kiwanis Club had a field day at the Madison camp grounds, and they asked me to make the coffee. They said they wanted good coffee, and I could have any kind I wanted. I told them to go to the A&P store and buy ten pounds of their cheapest bulk coffee. They were afraid that wouldn't be good enough, but they got it, and I used it—five pounds in a bag to each of two wash boilers. Everyone crowded around for more of that delicious coffee. People who didn't know where the coffee was bought came over to my store and asked to buy the same kind I used at the picnic.

The truth is—you want to use some coffee. My wife used to say, "You make the coffee; you make it better than I do." The reason was simple—the recipe called for a handful of coffee and mine was the bigger hand. Grange and lodge committees come in and buy two or three pounds of coffee and feed the multitude. Five pounds would be better—maybe ten. And if they use cheap bulk coffee it won't cost anymore than paying the extra tariff on a brand name for a pound or so less.

## CORN BREAD, ETC.

I heard a professor of economics speak one time, and he told us the small retail grocery store was doomed because no one could afford to pay thirty-two cents a pound for coffee when the chain store sold it for seventeen cents. The man was a victim of a rather gigantic delusion. The chain stores sell bulk coffee, most small retailers handle heavily advertised packaged brands. Unfortunately, few grocers see this difference and fewer still try to remedy it. I have always enjoyed a good coffee trade because I pushed bulk varieties and as often as not could sell cheaper than the chains.

There is a difference in coffees—but I believe most people would be stumped to explain it. The elevation at which a coffee grows affects the flavor, and mountainous sections have the best reputations. But most coffee today is blended—whether cheap or expensive. Most coffee, today, is like the port wine I sold Mrs. Hanan. I believe nowhere in the whole food picture is the public's gullibility better shown than in buying coffee. Advertising has them completely bewildered, and they buy advertising instead of coffee. If the small retail grocers would buy a good grade of bulk coffee, grind it daily, and sell it at a fair profit they'd get back the business they have lost to highly advertised brands. The matter is important to the grocer, because he can make more on a cheap bulk coffee than he can on an expensive packaged brand.

A Spanish recipe for coffee says it must be as pure as an angel, as sweet as love, as black as the devil, and as hot as hell. Most Americans think it must also support a radio program, come in a sealed can, and tell the time.

Anyway—the years have rolled by, and our food products have changed. High pressure publicity, nourishment fads,

## CORN BREAD, ETC.

packaging, the development of by-products, and a hundred other things have contrived to change the quality of things we can put on our shelves. I won't say modern products are poorer—it is personal opinion that the old-time products tasted better. One by one I have seen new articles move onto my counters, and every now and then some grandmotherly customer reads a label and says, "I doubt it's as good."

It is curious, too, that the modern foods in their party dresses pay a smaller profit to the storekeeper. The chain store technique had its effect in forcing many such goods on all retailers. The majority of storekeepers felt they had no other course. For my own part, I think I'd rather have stuck to the old-time products could I have still got them. I think I could do well today with a hogshead of real molasses. I think I could find customers for some ground and unbolted meal. As for coffee, I know the highly advertised brands can be licked on the home front by any enterprising merchant who tries to do it.

Once in a while I had a chance to see it work. I have related how I sold soap without handling P&G—I licked them in my territory simply because I couldn't do business with their product and make a profit. I no doubt lost some deluded customers who still thought the advertised brand was best—but as far as soap went I wasn't making anything on them anyway.

We handled a bleaching compound that was much advertised—a mixture to wash clothes with. The compound wasn't any great secret, and wasn't protected in any way. I had a high school boy analyze it for me in chemistry class. Because it was advertised on billboards all over the state everyone

## CORN BREAD, ETC.

thought it was wonderful. I made some of it once, stirring it up in a big cauldron down cellar. A salesman asked for me upstairs, and the bookkeeper said I was downstairs making a big stink. The salesman came down and found me stirring the stuff and weeping at the ammonia in it.

I bottled it and gave away the first batch as samples. I told the women it was better than anything else, and suggested they compare it with the advertised brand. Most of them said mine was better. So I have reason to believe the high school chemist did his job well, and I followed his suggestions unerringly. I sold the stuff for years, a few cents cheaper, and the profit took my breath away full as well as the ammonia.

Advertised pre-cooked meats are likely to be made of scraps. They don't have to be inferior meat—just scraps. Using good quality scraps, I made some pre-cooked meat just like that we bought. Nobody could tell the difference—and if they bought mine they found the price somewhat cheaper. I made vanilla extract for years—synthetic, of course, but it sold and it paid a smart penny.

The jump from corn bread to synthetic vanilla is really a small distance. Products in the store are valuable only when they sell and return a profit on the investment. Quality is not always a criterion with the customer. They pay for packages, they pay for brands, they pay for slogans. If they bought quality, and insisted on it—we'd still get decent molasses. If they allowed their grocer—as their purchasing agent—to tell them right from wrong, we'd see a very differently appearing market. And yet things have gone so far that the storekeepers themselves are either confused, or they find no choice but to string along with the trend.

## CORN BREAD, ETC.

The funniest aspect of all is the disliking the public has for allowing the grocer a profit. I think people trade at chain stores because they think the chains make less on a given article. In theory, this is undoubtedly so—but in general and in the long run it isn't. They make a profit, and don't forget it. They simply have a different way of arriving at it. If I sell a standard packaged item, I am expected to match prices with every store in town. All right—that's because you are buying a package.

But if you want a value—the chances are that I can give you just as good a product, sometimes with no name on it at all, and the price will make your eyeballs stick out a foot. But to be honest with me—how many of you have ever asked your grocer to take his hair down and tell what he knows?

## 23

## CO-OPS AND CHAIN STORES

A SMART independent merchant can make money in competition with either cooperative or chain grocery stores. Not only that, but he can have a lot of fun making them squirm. To be sure, a good many storekeepers are clever enough merchandisers to merit this pleasure—but as many others are unequal to the occasion, and from them come most of the complaints. In the face of active, smart, and steady competition the chain or co-op is at such a disadvantage that it isn't funny for the poor managers.

Shortly after I bought at Harmony a man came in and told me I'd have to take down my sign. "They'll drive you out of business," he said. "They've organized a consumer's cooperative."

I asked him who was at the head of it, and when I heard the name I said I guessed I'd stick around a little longer, anyway. I wondered at the time just what ramification of business would be too much for them. It turned out to be corn.

They came out in November with a price on new corn. I

## CO-OPS AND CHAIN STORES

was still selling old corn, and at that time they didn't have any corn at all. Well, their price on new corn was 10 cents a bag under mine—and although I was invited to consider this horrible situation, I continued to sell corn. A store without corn can quote any price it wants to. Their car of corn arrived in January, and by that time I had bought new corn and my price was cheaper than theirs. It ruined the thing right there. The farmers canceled their orders, with some bad feeling all around, and they came over to my place and bought corn.

The cooperative is usually a dreaming group of inexperienced people who are taken in by the notion they can save money. The nature of the organization places their store manager under such handicaps he can't do the right kind of a job. They have an initial difficulty in getting the right man to run the store. If he is the right man, he usually has a better job than the co-op can offer him. But if they do get him, they hedge him in so with committees and trustees that he can't act soon enough to take advantage of market conditions. Nearly as often they get the wrong man and then don't supervise him enough. The cooperative can be successful with the right man behind it. But with another good man working for himself across the street, they are usually doomed before they start. The idea is good, and I've often thought I'd like to manage a co-op somewhere and show the members how it could be done.

The chain store is another proposition. Here you have shrewd buying and careful merchandising, and coupled with great buying capacity this makes hard competition. But the chain store has its weaknesses. First of all, it is not a local

## CO-OPS AND CHAIN STORES

store. People in the small towns are folksy, and as long as things look right to them they'll stick with the local man. No chain-store manager can ever get as close to his trade as the hometown owner, even if the manager is a hometown boy himself.

There was plenty of bad blood between the independents and the chains when the A&P, First National, Helpy-Selfy, and similar ideas worked back into the sticks. Many a neighborhood dealer in the suburbs went out of business. But out in the country the chains met another kind of man—the rural trader who knew a thing or two himself.

One store came in near me, and they'd plaster their windows with loss leaders every week. My customers rubbed it in pretty hard. I knew what things cost, and knew the chain was fooling the people with prices under cost. So I watched the chain, and every week I'd plaster my front with the same thing they'd advertised the week before. Only I'd offer it for a cent or two less. Usually everyone had stocked up the week before, and I didn't have to sell much—but I did make the chain mad. More than that, I made some of my customers mad at the chain.

In 1920 I made them so mad they haven't forgotten it. Sugar has been thirty-four cents a pound, and it broke overnight to eight cents. The chains, of course, had a big stock because of their mass buying. I wasn't investing heavily in thirty-four-cent sugar, so when the price broke I ran in some eight-cent sugar so fast I was afraid it was going to caramel in the car. The chains were still trying to sell sugar at twenty-five cents when the Madison *Bulletin* came out with my ad in it:

## CO-OPS AND CHAIN STORES

> David and Goliath had an awful fight
> Over how much sugar for a dollar.
> David picked up a brick
> And hit Goliath such a lick,
> That a man in North Anson heard him holler.

The manager promptly went mad, and nobody in the whole area sold sugar for more than eight cents after that. For months, whenever I felt low over anything at all, I'd think of the thirty-four-cent sugar I made the chain sell for eight cents—and the world was suddenly lovely and kind.

One point on which the chains fall down is the realization that small-profits-big-turnover means a lot more running around. They don't seem to realize that if they can sell one article and make ninety cents on it, they've done just as well as they do when they sell ten articles and make nine cents on each. They train their clerks in display and selling—but they don't usually make their costs available, and the clerks don't know what to push. I always push the item that carries the bigger profit. A chain-store clerk knows selling prices—but not cost prices. The storekeeper must always know both—and never forget them as long as trade is in the store.

I was in New York one time and a salesman said, "Mr. Gould, you ought to buy a dozen of these Waldemar vest chains—genuine fire gilt and warranted. We have a man on the East Side who buys a dozen every morning—and before night he's sold them all for ninety-eight cents each." I asked the price, and in a voice calculated to fill me with wonder he said, "Sixty-five cents a dozen."

I told him if the chain stores ever put me out of the grocery

## CO-OPS AND CHAIN STORES

business I'd give his chains a whirl. The independent merchant can change his line overnight if it fails to yield a profit. On the other hand, a chain manager can't do a thing about local conditions until he has orders from a boss in some distant city. That fact alone gives the local man a great advantage. It's a grand feeling when I wake up in the morning with a good idea and put it across before noon the same day —and then spend three days watching the chain manager sweat until he gets orders from headquarters.

The lack of knowledge of local conditions on the part of chain organization is well known to all chain managers. When I took on a gasoline distributing agency for my territory, I found out just what that means. The office in New York was always raising Ned about stock loss. They didn't know anything about weather conditions up here—but I did. Gasoline shrinks about .007 for every degree in temperature. Thus it follows that if a car is loaded at 50 degrees and unloaded at $-40$ degrees, we have a factor of $63 \times 10,000$ gallons—or 630 gallons shrinkage. The mathematics didn't puzzle them—they knew that. They just didn't believe the thermometer ever went down that far.

Once when I recorded a temperature of $-56$ degrees in my territory, they sent an auditor up post-haste. He pointed at my figure and said, "Have you anything to prove this?" I dug out a copy of the *Bulletin* which said, "The temperature at the Great Northern Paper Co. was 56 below Wednesday morning, but it was much colder in the country." He took this back to New York, and I didn't hear so much about temperature.

Another thing they used to do was send me all sorts of

## CO-OPS AND CHAIN STORES

printed matter designed to help me sell gasoline in my territory. I was supposed to ask the customer, "Fill it up?" with a rising inflection. I was supposed to suggest a change of oil, etc., etc. I was reading it when honk, honk, out front brought me to my feet, and I rushed out somewhat bemused and inquired, "Fill it up?" "Nope," he said. "Just gimme two quarts. I only got ten cents."

There was a lot more of the same, but it goes to show how a centralized management falls short of sizing up local conditions. However, when a chain store tries to merchandise me out of business they've got a lot of things to consider. One is that I am a buyer as well as a seller, and it is possible for me to go on making a living year after year regardless of my grocery inventory. I have bought two woodlots, resold them to an operator, and made a year's business on that single exchange. I'll buy anything I think I can sell at a profit. It doesn't do any good to set a trap unless you tend it. In my own home town I've got a better trapline than the chains.

I have, however, envied them some of the things they can do. A while ago, the chain stores began selling a new brand of mustard. It seems the western grain fields were infested with wild mustard, a weed, and the grain elevators charged two cents a bushel to clean the grain. A new concern put in an outfit and began cleaning grain for one cent a bushel. In the course of time this new concern began grinding and packing mustard for chain stores. It was mustard, all right—but not the English white mustard grown and cultivated for its seed and handled by experienced spice merchants.

Some years ago I was in the office of *Grocer's Magazine*, in Boston, and the editor told me I should have been in the day

## CO-OPS AND CHAIN STORES

before. "A most interesting man was here," he said. "A doctor of sick business for the A&P." Whenever a store failed to show a profit this man was sent around to find out why. He had just spent a month in a supermarket in a suburb, and the store was showing a profit when he got through.

"What did he find?" I asked.

"Oh, a lot of little things. The lights were all on one switch, and whoever got there first pulled the switch and the lights burned all day. They paid $300 a month. Then they had a big laundry bill on the white coats they supply the clerks. Clerks would grab a clean frock every hour or so. Now each clerk gets two clean ones a week, and if he uses more than that he has to pay the laundry bill himself. Then there was a lot more like that."

I said, "It doesn't take a very smart man to be doctor of business for the A&P, does it?"

The editor said, "That occurred to me, too."

A lot of small leaks will sink a ship. The small dealer with all the strings in his hands can watch every cent, and make a living wage in the small leaks.

So I never worried much about the co-ops and chains. I've seen them come—and I've seen some of them go. They survive only as long as they follow sound business practices. An independent merchant who tries to drive them out of business bites off quite a chunk—but he can make a living alongside of them. They have their advantages, and they are hard to overcome. But they have their disadvantages, and by capitalizing on them the independent can have a rather pleasant income.

## 24

## TWO PERCENT, TEN DAYS

WE AREN'T bothered so much by them now, but there was a time that city slicker bond-and-stock salesmen circulated about the countryside with business opportunities calculated to make a man's eyes bug out like frankfurters. They always headed for my store, and I'd occasionally give them a hearing. One chap was giving me the works one afternoon and I stopped him. "Look here, feller," I said, "I've got a far better proposition that anything you ever heard of. I'd be foolish to invest money with you."

"What is it?" he asked.

I said, "Two percent ten days, net 30 days." He didn't get it, and neither do a lot of people. You just figure up what you can do with $100 if you discount bills with it every ten days—$6 a month, $72 a year. It can't be beaten. If a storekeeper has a big enough business, he can sell goods at cost and take his profit in the discount the wholesaler allows him for ten-day settling. Two percent every ten days is better than six percent compounded semi-annually.

## TWO PERCENT, TEN DAYS

On only one occasion in my lifetime did I try to step out of character and indulge in big business. Once was enough. A biscuit company was expanding, going to build a new bakery at Portland, and they were issuing some eight percent preferred stock that I could get. I'd done business with the company, knew their product was good, so I bought a block of stock and sat back to become wealthy. I got a few dividend checks, and then I didn't get any. As I've said, I think it pays to tend a trapline, so I began to investigate. I uncovered some peculiar information, but they wouldn't give me a list of stockholders or let me look at the books. So I brought suit to compel the officers of the corporation to let me see the books. I had a pretty good lawyer, and there was a state law that seemed to make me on the right side. The hearing came before Chief Justice Cornish at Augusta, and I put on my other clothes and went down to state with my case.

I told the judge the story and he nodded all the time. He seemed to appreciate my position. I cited the law in question, whereat he nodded all the harder. Finally he broke in:

"I know that law—I drafted it when I was in legislature, and it was written to give relief to people in your very situation. Now I believe every word you've spoken is the truth, and I find you've complied with the law. I shall issue the order asked for."

As we walked out of the court house I told my lawyer, "I suppose they'll appeal." He said, "Appeal? On what grounds? It must be on the law or evidence. He put that in on purpose about believing what you said. The judge that wrote the law sat on the case—they couldn't appeal if they wanted to in the face of the evidence you gave. They won't appeal."

## TWO PERCENT, TEN DAYS

They didn't. I got my order, and then the officers began giving me the high finance routine. They showed me a lot of meaningless figures, and frequently indicated they thought they'd get around me in time. But we uncovered an issue of $500,000 of common stock to the president of the company in exchange for the right to use the words "Pine Tree Cookies" which he had copyrighted in his own name. After that it was easier. We met with the corporation's lawyers, and before long we had an arrangement all figured out.

One of the stockholders on my side was an old minister in Effingham, New Hampshire, and he finally wrote and said he had been offered $35 a share for his stock, and he thought he'd sell, because it didn't seem likely he'd ever get more than that. I told him if he wanted to sell to send me his certificates and I'd buy them for that—but I thought if he'd hold off two weeks he'd do better.

In a week we were awarded $80 a share. The minister wrote and thanked me. He said he and his wife could never reward me as I deserved, but they had talked it over and decided they would both pray for me every night as long as they both lived. This anchor to windward was about all I got out of my only intrusion into the realm of high finance—and perhaps it was better than the million dollars I thought I was going to get. Anyway, I went back to my own methods of making a living and gave added attention to the soundest investment I've ever known—two percent discount in ten days.

## 25

## THE OLD ORDERS CHANGE

It was about 1925 that I noticed business decreasing and felt it was time to accommodate myself to new things. At first I couldn't figure it out. I noticed fruit sales fell off. I mentioned this to another storekeeper, and he said he'd noticed the same thing. I thought the chain stores were getting the business, but the managers said they were losing on that, too. I asked one of my drivers, "How long since you've had a Sunday dinner order?"

He said he hadn't seen one for over a year. We used to get ten or twenty every week—big orders for Sunday dinners that would come to five or ten dollars each. The change had come, all right—but it was hard to figure it out. Sunday dinner orders now were more likely to be a bottle of Moxie, a can of sardines, some crackers, and ten gallons of gasoline. It is a fact that gasoline had changed our eating habits.

Other things had, too—of course. Commodities had changed—the package goods era was on us; foods were getting to be of the three-minute kind—easy to prepare, easy to serve, easy to digest, easy to everything. Living habits in gen-

## THE OLD ORDERS CHANGE

eral had changed. And change is the hardest thing in the world for a Yankee.

But the old days never come again, and I knew soon afterward that the old days of the country storekeeper were done. Thousands, with purely nostalgic sentiment, have lamented the passing of the old country store scene. Once in a while they find an old shop that retains some of the bygone features —but even in their similarity they are far different from the days I knew. Once in a while a man can eat, even today, buckets of mulberry mixture, real corned hake, true-to-life common crackers, time-ripened cheese, and even Congress boots for the old men in town.

But these things were only part of the story. The hustle and bustle that went with handling things like that is behind us. Trading is no longer a weekly adventure, requiring the packing of crates of eggs, wiping off the molasses jug, making a long list of items, and coming down to the village with nothing in mind whatever but getting a good price and stocking up for the week ahead.

I made my change before conditions made it for me. I went into the wholesale gasoline business, and cornered my end of the state. You'll find my pumps up north of Eustis, at the international boundary where Canadians start down over the Arnold Trail from Quebec. I've converted, and find the change agreeable to my increasing age and laziness. Then I went into woodlots. In whittling down my store accounts I found a number of able-bodied men owed me—and I put them to chopping wood.

Even that, however, has changed. We used to sell wood green to people who worked it up and stacked it in sheds for

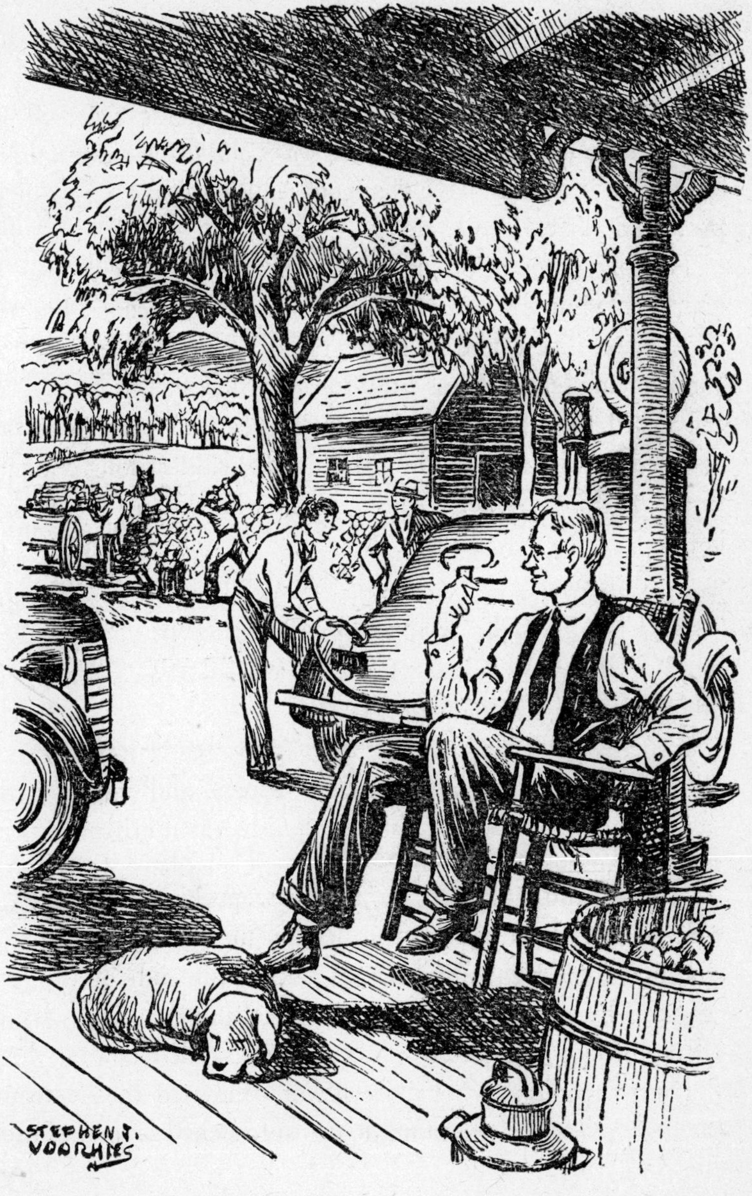
STEPHEN J.
VOORHIES

## THE OLD ORDERS CHANGE

the winter. Now they telephone in for two feet of wood and "Hurry, because the last stick is in the stove." I still keep a few groceries on the shelves, and am about as eager for a good stroke of business as I ever was. But I am older, and I am lazier, and times have changed. And if I don't see a quick profit I don't care to trade.

The big corporation can amortize its investment over a couple of hundred years. The country storekeeper has to investigate, invest, and make his profit all in his own lifetime. I am having less and less time for each new venture.

I heard the other day about a high school principal who resigned and bought a store. My idea is he'll last long enough to realize his mistake. I think a man who doesn't know any better than to buy a store these days is well removed from our educational system. And in that connection I might pass on a few words of wisdom that came to me from an old fellow in town who stopped in recently to buy some eating tobacco.

He said he noticed I was tapering off my store business. I said yes—I was getting old and times had changed. He said, "I suppose you'll go to raising hens?"

I said I might get me a few.

"Well," and Solomon himself was speaking, "most men who leave a store go into the hen business. If you're smart, you'll go into it easy like. Don't put nothin' into it till you get something out of it. Borrow a setting hen and buy a setting of eggs and hatch some chickens, and that way when you get a thousand hens you'll know how to take care of them. If you put a thousand dollars into hens and hen houses

## THE OLD ORDERS CHANGE

and incubators and brooders, in a few years you'll have some brooders and incubators to sell—and no money."

I know there exist a great many young people who fancy they'd like to own a store. I have made a good living in a store, and maybe I can be permitted to pass on a word of advice: Start with a setting of eggs—the quickest way in the world to lose money is to try a business about which you know nothing.

It's too bad I can't keep on as a Yankee storekeeper—it's been a lot of fun. But the gasoline and wood business has its amusing moments, too, and every once in a while I get a chance to use to advantage the tricks I've learned from my father on the farm, from my customers in the store, and from the smart city drummers determined to sell me a pile of goods big enough to choke a horse.